— The —

North Shore
LITERARY
TRAIL

The
North Shore
LITERARY
TRAIL

From

BRADSTREET'S ANDOVER

to

HAWTHORNE'S SALEM

Kristin Bierfelt

Charleston   London

THE
History
PRESS

Published by The History Press
Charleston, SC 29403
www.historypress.net

Copyright © 2009 by Kristin Bierfelt
All rights reserved

All images are © Jeff Steward unless otherwise noted.

Cover design Marshall Hudson and Natasha Momberger

First published 2009

Manufactured in the United States

ISBN 978.1.59629.520.9

Library of Congress Cataloging-in-Publication Data

Bierfelt, Kristin.
The North Shore literary trail : from Bradstreet's Andover to Hawthorne's Salem
/ Kristin Bierfelt.
p. cm.
Includes bibliographical references and index.
ISBN 978-1-59629-520-9
1. Literary landmarks--Massachusetts--North Shore (Coast)--Guidebooks. 2.
Literary landmarks--Massachusetts--Boston Region--Guidebooks. 3. Authors,
American--Homes and haunts--Massachusetts--North Shore (Coast) 4. Authors,
American--Homes and haunts--Massachusetts--Boston Region. 5. American
literature--Massachusetts--North Shore (Coast)--History and criticism. 6.
American literature--Massachusetts--Boston Region--History and criticism. 7.
North Shore (Mass. : Coast)--History, Local. 8. North Shore (Mass. : Coast)--
Intellectual life. 9. Boston Region (Mass.)--History, Local. 10. Boston Region
(Mass.)--Intellectual life. I. Title.
PS144.N64B54 2009
810.9'9744--dc22

2008050260

Contents

CONTENTS

PREFACE

Perhaps the best-known and most continuously read author from the North Shore is Nathaniel Hawthorne, hailed by even his ardent critic Edgar Allan Poe as "one of the few men of indisputable genius to whom our country has as yet given birth"[1] and considered one of the first distinctly American—rather than British or colonial—literary voices. However, Hawthorne was preceded and is followed by scores of other local voices, from the revolutionary to the quietly influential, from the canonical to the footnote, all of whom contributed a unique piece to the quilt of North Shore arts and culture.

The North Shore of Boston and the Merrimack Valley to the northwest are home to towns where fishermen and antiques shop owners sit side by side at town meetings, where stables and lacrosse fields share borders with working family farms and where former factory towns look to artists and immigrant communities as a way to revitalize architecturally significant downtowns in a postindustrial age.

As different as these towns can be, they are all quintessential New England and share a history that encompasses religious tolerance and social persecution, conflict and cooperation with Native Americans and a resourceful, respectful relationship with the land and sea that even modern residents need to cultivate in order to weather long, northern winters.

Essex County in 1856, by Henry Francis Walling. *Courtesy Norman B. Leventhal Map Center at the Boston Public Library.*

Visitors come to soak up the early American history. Pioneering settlers moved north to expand the borders of the Massachusetts Bay Colony; some of their homes still stand in towns like Ipswich. The witch hysteria that gripped Salem in 1692 continues to fascinate, making that modern-day city one of the most popular destinations in New England and fueling scholars' research, as well as novelists' imaginations, ever since. The story of the United States' transition from farming to manufacturing is told over and over again in the architecture of Merrimack Valley towns—massive former mills that drew young women away from farm life in the early 1800s but now sit empty or await transformation into modern office buildings and apartments. The incomparable landscape also beckons. From leisurely rowing along the Essex River to the rough waters faced by Gloucester fishermen, northeastern Massachusetts is shaped by the sea.

The region's many architectural highlights add to the spirit of living, working and playing on the North Shore. Ipswich contains more First Period (approximately 1626 through 1725) houses than any other town in the country—and more than half of all that still exist in the country.[2] Lowell and Lawrence are both industrial boomtowns that are transforming former textile mills into cutting-edge artist's lofts while making room for a growing Caribbean and Central and South American community. The Federal-era mansions in downtown Salem speak to that town's years of being a leading seaport and home base for many merchant captains. The winding streets and narrow alleys of Marblehead are anything but cookie-cutter, and they fuel the imagination with ideas of what life may have been like in these villages when streets were built to accommodate horses and buggies rather than trucks and buses.

February skies over a frozen Ipswich salt marsh. © *Rachel Rowe*.

A commuter rail train pulling in to the Montserrat stop in Beverly. © *Brian Lewandowski, bglewandowski.com.*

And while Boston and Concord to the south may claim higher name recognition for their native authors, essayists and poets, the North Shore and Merrimack Valley have a rich literary history waiting to be discovered. Whether you're planning a literary-themed cultural outing or just want to take closer note of local landmarks in your hometown, this book will uncover the North Shore's hidden literary history, as well as put its biggest luminaries in context.

In some cases, you can visit the very homes where some of our nation's most important early authors were born and raised, such as the John Greenleaf Whittier Homestead in Haverhill and Nathaniel Hawthorne's birthplace at the House of the Seven Gables museum in Salem. Other authors, such as Anne Bradstreet in the seventeenth century, passed through the North Shore and left little but their influence and legacy behind.

There is also a generation gap in this guide. Few authors who were active in the early part of the twentieth century are included in these pages, and this is in part because of the cycle of history. Authors who were extremely popular in their time are often forgotten as the generation who first read them passes on, and they are not rediscovered until scholars begin to understand their writing as part of a bigger picture. With the notable exception of John Greenleaf Whittier—who was still alive and working while various admiration societies were active—few of these historic homes and landmarks were established while writers were still alive. Of the contemporary authors included here, only time will tell if their current homes and haunts will become stops on the next generation's tour of local literary history.

Whether retracing an author's footsteps and peering in at her parlor or noticing drastic changes between a town as a poet chronicled it and as it now appears, it is my hope that this guide will open your eyes to the breadth of literary culture that flourishes in northeast Massachusetts, as it has done for more than 350 years.

ACKNOWLEDGEMENTS

This book grew out of the Escapes North literary itinerary featured at www.escapesnorth.com, which I wrote with Bonnie Hurd Smith in 2007 under the auspices of Julie McConchie at the North of Boston Convention and Visitors Bureau and Elaine Aliberti at the Peabody Essex Museum. Escapes North is a cultural tourism program in Essex County led by those two organizations, with support from the Massachusetts Cultural Council.

Thanks to my husband, Jeff Steward, for accompanying me, camera in hand, on many research trips to the North Shore. I am grateful to my mother, Elizabeth Bierfelt, and my aunt, Nancy Carl, for their feedback on an early version of this book. And thanks to Saunders Robinson at The History Press for all of her suggestions as the book took shape.

GLOUCESTER

As America's oldest seaport, life in Gloucester has been shaped by the tides since the town was first incorporated in 1642. The rocky land was ill suited for anything but family farms, and until the eighteenth century, fishing was mostly done close to shore and on a small scale. In fact, the town green was more than two miles away from the waterfront, and it wasn't until two hundred years later that the harbor became the focal point of Gloucester life.

Early settlers cleared huge sections of the inland forest to use the land for pasture, creating the area called Dogtown, which became a hardscrabble—some say haunted—settlement and has now been reclaimed by the forest. Anita Diamant's 2005 novel *The Last Days of Dogtown* chronicles just that. Now a ghost town, few accurate records of the village's history remain, but legends of witches, widows and wild women abound. As Diamant notes in her introduction, her fictional creations were often inspired by Charles E. Mann's 1906 volume *In the Heart of Cape Ann or the Story of Dogtown*, itself based on little more than gossip gleaned from the few Gloucester residents old enough to remember Dogtown when it was still inhabited.

Today, Dogtown is a jumble of trails and old cellar holes, dotted with the large boulders that made the area so inhospitable to farming. Many of the boulders now bear often cryptic carved mottoes—such as "If Work Stops Values Decay" and "Help

One of Roger Babson's boulder carvings in Dogtown Commons, Gloucester. *Courtesy Wikimedia Commons.*

Mother"—commissioned during the Depression by businessman Roger Babson. In 1935, he wrote in his book *Actions and Reactions*:

> *My family says that I am defacing the boulders and disgracing the family with these inscriptions, but the work gives me a lot of satisfaction, fresh air, exercise and sunshine. I am really trying to write a simple book with words carved in stone instead of printed paper.*

As the shipbuilding industry grew, so did Gloucester's role as a center of the commercial fishing industry. One of the most accessible North Atlantic fishing ports, Gloucester sits at the center coast of George's Banks, an elevated area of the seafloor extending from Cape Cod to Nova Scotia. Thousands of emigrants from the Azores and Sicily arrived in the eighteenth century to work in the fisheries, and their cultural influence remains strong in tightknit church congregations and social clubs, as well as through the traditional Portuguese and Italian cuisine available at restaurants, bakeries and neighborhood groceries. Rudyard Kipling's 1897 novel *Captains Courageous* provides an outsider's look at a Gloucester-based Portuguese fishing crew through the eyes of a spoiled young man whom the crew has the misfortune to rescue at sea.

Advances in meteorology, communication and satellite-aided navigation have made life on the sea much safer than in the mid-nineteenth century, when more than 4,000 men were lost over a 60-year stretch. "Since 1623, when the British first set up their camp just across the harbor, perhaps 10,000 Gloucester men have gone down to the sea. That's one fisherman lost every 13 days for 375 years," notes radio host Sandy Tolan.[3] But technology is also moving the industry away from Gloucester, as more commercial fisheries become part of large international corporations. The men and women who continue to make their livings on the sea are a close community, and any loss is deeply felt by the town's residents. The most widely known tragedy in recent history was the sinking of the *Andrea Gail* and the loss of its six crewmen during an exceptional nor'easter in October 1991. Sebastian Junger's 1997 book about the event, *The Perfect Storm*, did more to bring contemporary Gloucester into the light than any other recent work. Stop for a drink at the Crow's Nest on 334 Main Street and you're likely to take a stool next to folks who vividly remember the storm and can also tell you what it was like when Hollywood took over the waterfront to shoot the film version of Junger's book in 2000.

The difference between the visitors' Gloucester and the natives' Gloucester can be vast. Photographer Lynn Swigart, in his book *Olson's Gloucester*, writes that the city, "small as it is, is a honeycomb of roads that people have to tell you about; the signs say Private or Keep Out, but the natives can go there all the time—you have to learn all those things or you can't even find the real city."[4] Historian Joe Garland alludes to the same spirit in his book of "rambles," *The Gloucester Guide*: "This is not really a guide to Gloucester at all. No one is guided through our myriad city, only beguiled by it. Gloucester is here, and if you would savor her, you will do so on her

Sculptor Leonard Craske's *Man at the Wheel* at Gloucester's harborside honors "They that go down to the sea in ships." © *Paul Keleher*.

terms, not via the megaphone of any tour director." As always, one of the best ways to explore a city is by seeing it through the eyes of its authors. The authors that follow are a perfect place to start.

JUDITH SARGENT MURRAY (1751—1820)

A sensible and informed woman—companionable and serious—
possessing also a facility of temper, and united to a congenial
mind—blest with competency—and rearing to maturity a promising
family of children—Surely, the wide globe cannot produce a scene
more truly interesting.
—Judith Sargent Murray in The Gleaner,
Volume III, No. LXXXVIII

Judith Sargent Murray was one of America's first strong feminist voices. A lifelong Gloucester resident, she was not tutored like her Harvard-bound brother, but she did have full access to the family's abundant library. She voraciously read the classics and learned Greek and Latin. She also had her father's support from an early age and continued to underline the importance of early education as a key to achieving women's equality. Through her essays, she developed a powerful public voice on behalf of women and female writers as she urged the new American nation to improve the status of education, economic independence and political rights for women. She was also a poet, playwright and editor, publishing her own work and editing the sermons, letters and autobiography of her second husband, the prominent Universalist leader John Murray.

Using the pen name Constantia, Judith Sargent Murray published the essay "On the Equality of the Sexes" in *Massachusetts Magazine*'s March and April 1790 installments. This highly respected periodical reached the entire eastern seaboard and across the Atlantic to England, and Murray's essay predates Mary Wollstonecraft's better-known "Vindication of the Rights of Woman" by two years. Adopting a male persona, Murray also wrote the popular series "The Gleaner" for *Massachusetts Magazine*. Later, she became the first woman in America to self-publish a book (*The Gleaner*, 1798) and the first American to have a play produced in Boston (*The Medium*, 1795).

Murray also kept letter books throughout her adult life with the intention of creating an archive for future generations. Although this was a common practice with male politicians, authors and clergymen, historians believe that Murray's collection of approximately five thousand pieces of correspondence is the only one of its kind by a woman of her era. The books' existence was unknown until a Universalist minister found them in 1984 in Natchez, Mississippi, where Murray moved two years before her death to be closer to her daughter. Historian Bonnie Hurd Smith began the arduous task of transcribing and publishing the letter books for the Judith Sargent Murray Society in 1994.

The following quote is taken from "On the Equality of the Sexes":

> *Yes, ye lordly, ye haughty sex, our souls are by nature equal to yours; the same breath of God animates, enlivens, and invigorates us...I dare confidently believe, that from the commencement of time to the present day, there hath been as many females, as males, who, by the mere force of natural powers, have merited the crown of applause; who, thus assisted, have seized the wreath of fame.*

PLACES TO SEE

64 Middle Street, Gloucester
This was the home of Murray's in-laws through her first marriage to John Stevens. The young couple lived here until their own house was built on an adjacent lot.

Sargent House Museum, 49 Middle Street, Gloucester
Judith Sargent Murray's first husband, John Stevens, built this Georgian mansion in 1782, eight years before her essay "On the Equality of the Sexes" was published. The couple only lived here together for four years before John fled his creditors and sailed to the West Indies. He died there in 1787, and Judith married the Universalist minister John Murray. They lived here for the first six years of their marriage before moving to Boston in 1794. The

Hough family owned the house for the next one hundred years until Gloucester's Universalist community, along with members of the Sargent family—including Judith's great-great nephew, the renowned portraitist John Singer Sargent—opened it to the public in 1917. The collection includes work by colonial silversmiths John Burt and Paul Revere, furniture made in Newburyport and French wallpaper given by John Singer Sargent.

Virginia Lee Burton (1909–1968)

Children's book author and illustrator Virginia Lee Burton grew up in Newton Center, west of Boston, with her mother, who was a poet and musician, and her father, the first dean of the Massachusetts Institute of Technology. She spent her adolescence in California and eventually enrolled in art school. On the long ferryboat ride from home in Alameda to school in San Francisco, she drew portraits of fellow commuters and credits this experience with helping her land her first job as a "sketcher" for the *Boston Transcript*. By then, she had returned to the East to help her aging father and had enrolled in artist George Demetrios's drawing class at the Boston Museum School. After a short classroom courtship, she and Demetrios were married the following spring.

The couple moved to the Folly Cove neighborhood of Gloucester, where both were active in the local arts community. It was after this move that Burton (known as Jinnee to friends and family) began writing children's books. Her first attempt was unsuccessful, as she writes:

> *My first book,* Jonnifer Lint, *was about a piece of dust. I and my friends thought it was very clever but thirteen publishers disagreed with us and when I finally got the manuscript back and read it to* [my son] *Aris, age three and a half, he went to sleep before I could even finish it. That taught me a lesson*

and from then on I worked with and for my audience, my own children.[5]

Her most enduring work is *Mike Mulligan and His Steam Shovel*, which has been constantly in print since its debut in 1939. She won the Caldecott Medal for *The Little House* in 1942. Other volumes, including *Katy and the Big Snow*, about a tireless tractor, and *Maybelle the Cable Car*, which pays homage to Burton's school days in San Francisco, are both testaments to her decision to always write for her primary audience—her sons, Aristides and Michael.

In addition to her work as a children's author, Burton also founded a group that became known as the Folly Cove Designers, which grew out of a design course that she taught in her home studio. After creating fabric designs for exhibition and for retail from 1938 to 1970 (a year after Burton's death), the group donated its materials, sample books and tools to the Cape Ann Historical Society in Gloucester.

PLACES TO SEE

Cape Ann Museum, 27 Pleasant Street, Gloucester
The Cape Ann Museum holds the most extensive collection of work by the Folly Cove Designers, including Burton, on display at the museum's Folly Cove Auditorium.

CHARLES OLSON (1910–1970)

I read Olson's Maximus *a lot, sit with it on the porch and scatter my way through.*
—*Poet Hoa Nguyen*[6]

To academia and history books, Charles Olson is closely associated with the experimental Black Mountain College in North Carolina and fellow poets Robert Creeley, Denise Levertov and Robert Duncan. But his relationship with Gloucester is at the center of much of his work, especially his epic *Maximus Poems*. After an early career in politics, during which he organized rallies on behalf of Franklin Delano Roosevelt, he finally settled in Gloucester, where he had spent his boyhood summers.

Born in Worcester in 1910, Olson studied literature at Wesleyan, Harvard and Yale Universities, where he absorbed the historical and linguistic trivia that peppered his speech and writing. He was well versed in archaeological and anthropological knowledge and could quote freely from Hittite and Mayan verse. He was influenced by both Ezra Pound and William Carlos Williams, poets with whom he proudly affiliated himself.

While teaching at Black Mountain, Olson read the poem "This House" by Vincent Ferrini and paid a visit to the Gloucester poet, starting what would become a lifelong, albeit contentious, friendship. The two men—Olson, well connected and expensively educated, and Ferrini, a self-taught former factory worker—fought through letters and verse over who was more properly Gloucester's

Winter waves at Rockport's Halibut Point State Park.

main scribe. Many of Olson's *Maximus* poems take the form of letters to Ferrini, and some include such harshly critical verses that it is difficult to imagine the friendship surviving.

However, it is Olson's position as a poet of the waterfront that most comes through in these volumes. The poem "I, Maximus of Gloucester, to You" contains the following request to St. Anthony, who preached the famous sermon to the fishes in Padua, and links Gloucester's thriving Italian-American fishing community to its ancient roots:

> *...o*
> *Anthony of Padua*
> *sweep low, o bless*

> *the roofs, the old ones, the gentle steep ones*
> *on whose ridge-poles the gulls sit, from which they depart,*

> *And the flake-racks*

> *of my city!*

A commanding presence at six feet, eight inches tall, he graciously, if reluctantly, received fans at his home, and a stream of important mid-century writers and artists made the trek to the small flat across from Stage Fork Park until his death in 1970.

PLACES TO SEE

28 Fort Square, Gloucester
Only a small plaque marks the Olsons' former home, which remains a private residence. Across the street is Stage Fort Park, the site of the city's first settlement in 1623. It is an excellent place to get a taste of the Gloucester landscape, and the welcoming center offers tourist information and directions.

Vincent Ferrini (1913–2007)

I don't consider myself a poet. I consider myself an alchemist. I want to change the structure of society and people so they can come across fulfilling their private lives.
—Vincent Ferrini[7]

A poet of both industrial Lynn and later, most fully, of seaside Gloucester, Vincent Ferrini remained a creative, active and opinionated influence on the North Shore for more than fifty years until his death in 2007. "We have many poets, but Vinnie was *the* poet," former Gloucester mayor John Bell was quoted as saying in the *Boston Globe*.

Ferrini was raised in Lynn's brickyards, the son of Italian immigrant workers in the city's shoe factories. His first volume, *No Smoke*, published in 1940, details the strikes, layoffs and struggles faced by poor shoe factory workers and showcases his lifelong sensitivity to social issues and injustices.

But it is Gloucester with which Ferrini is most closely associated. He moved to 3 Liberty Street with his first wife and three young children in 1948 and, in addition to writing, ran a small frame shop that fostered his connection to the local arts scene. In his autobiography, *Hermit of the Clouds*, he wrote that the freedom of being self-employed allowed him "to write when the poem is hot within." A fixture downtown and at community meetings in his fedora and ascot, he argued passionately for the preservation of Gloucester's working waterfront and, by extension, the close-knit fishing community it supported.

Places to See

3 Liberty Street, Gloucester
Ferrini's first home in Gloucester remains a private residence.

126 East Main Street, Gloucester
It was at this no-frills cottage in East Gloucester where Ferrini, following his second divorce, maintained a frame shop and lived until months before his death. It remains a private residence.

JOSEPH GARLAND (B. 1922)

Garland is the definitive historian of the North Shore.
—John Updike

The fourth of a line of New England doctors, Joe Garland chose the U.S. Army over Harvard (after being voted "most temperamental" in the class of 1940 at Roxbury Latin) and served with the Forty-fifth Infantry Division in Italy during World War II. After returning, Garland pursued the life of a journalist and historian and has since authored more than twenty books and two hundred articles. His first book, *Lone Voyager*, is the biography of Gloucester's famous fisherman, Howard Blackburn, who lost most of his hands and toes to frostbite during an 1883 winter storm but continued to set solo sailing records for the rest of his life. Garland's most recent book, *The Unknowns*, chronicles his own experiences in wartime Europe, but the bulk of his work has been in unearthing and sharing the stories of Gloucester, his longtime home.

Writing about his hometown and his hopes for its future, Garland says:

> *Among the first settlements in America, may this greatest of fishing ports in the Western Hemisphere, and perhaps world, remain characteristically charismatic in its union with sea, rock, and sky. But it will take a strong dose of uncharacteristic self-awareness—now that the outer world is beating at our doors—to pull it off.*
>
> *So leave us alone, rest of the world.*[8]

Jonathan Bayliss (b. 1926)

A close friend of poet and neighbor Charles Olson, Jonathan Bayliss's central work is a quartet of books that render Gloucester as a magical, fictionalized world. Bayliss's work switches between languages and draws on math and logic puzzles, as well as mythological allegories. In *Gloucesterbook*, the first to be published but second in the tetralogy, Gloucester, recast as Dogtown, abuts Mesopotamia and includes the mythic Markland, Vinland and Atlantis. His character Ipsissimus Charlemagne is based on Olson, although Charlemagne's pro-development standpoint is at odds with Olson's own fear that development and highways would ruin Gloucester.

All of Bayliss's novels are published by Protean Press and Basilicum Press but are also available for free download directly from the author at www.baylisswritings.net. The final book, *Gloucestermas*, is still in progress.

Gregory Gibson (b. 1945)

Owner of the much-respected Ten Pound Books in Gloucester, Gregory Gibson began a new life as a writer following the 1992 murder of his son during a shooting rampage at Simon's Rock College in Great Barrington, Massachusetts. The book he wrote about the murder, *Gone Boy*, was his attempt to understand how it could have happened and to make sense of the tangled fallout that followed. The *Boston Globe* wrote, "Gregory Gibson started out investigating the murder of his son. He came away with a story that rivals Mailer's best fiction." The book received extensive critical praise, and Gibson found the experience of writing it so rewarding that he determined to return to writing again, something he had set aside in favor of steadier work when raising his family in the 1970s and '80s.

PLACES TO SEE

Ten Pound Island Books, 77 Langsford Street, Gloucester
Gibson has run this small antiquarian and used bookstore in the Lanesville section of Gloucester since 1976. It specializes in old and rare nautical books, but you'll find books on all kinds of maritime and local subjects, as well as extremely knowledgeable staff.

IPSWICH

In 1633, John Winthrop Jr., son of the Massachusetts Bay Colony's governor, led a group of twelve men to a coastal Native American area called Agawam with the purpose of founding a new settlement in the wilderness. Winthrop stayed only one year to oversee the 1634 incorporation of the new town called Ipswich. Among Ipswich's early settlers were farmers and shipbuilders, as well as the poet Anne Bradstreet and preacher and author John Wise. Within twelve years of the town's founding, the population had grown to eight hundred, thanks in part to the fresh water, power and transportation opportunities offered by the rolling Ipswich River.

Fishing, farming and shipbuilding were the town's main occupations in its first century, and as the population increased, a saltworks, tannery and lace-making factories were added to the riverside landscape. Boats from the West Indies unloaded molasses at the distillery. During the Industrial Revolution, Ipswich became the home of the country's first stocking-making machine when one was smuggled from England in 1833. During the nineteenth century, stockings and lace became a prominent part of the local economy, but Ipswich remained a rural and residential country town. Today's population is only twelve thousand, although that number swells with summertime visitors, as tourism has become an ever-larger part of the area's economy.

Ipswich's Whipple House.

Encompassing thirty-three square miles, of which one-third is protected marshland and estuaries, Ipswich has a traditional New England town center, defined by Main and Market Streets. Today, many visitors come to Ipswich to see a glimpse of the past. The town has the largest concentration of First Period, or pre-1725, homes of anywhere in the country, and many of them are on High Street just a few blocks up the hill from the town center—making it a picturesque place to stroll. Most of these homes are private residences, so stick to the sidewalks. On a pleasant summer day, you'll find many folks tending their gardens and trimming their lawns. Most take pride in their historic houses and will be happy to tell you what they know of their building's past life. Say hello and strike up a conversation—local history as told by locals is one of the best ways to take the pulse of any town.

The Heard and Whipple Houses maintained by the Ipswich Historical Society offer seasonal tours and periodic exhibitions on town history through the centuries. The Trustees of Reservations maintain the gorgeous Crane Beach, open to the public, with five miles of dune hiking and sandbars that, during low tide, allow beachgoers to wade out far from shore into the cool Atlantic waters.

One of the greatest summertime pleasures in Ipswich is sitting outside at a clam shack with a cold can of soda and a stack of napkins and snacking on mouthwatering fresh-caught fried clams. In September, locals and visitors pack the yearly Chowderfest events to sample and celebrate the town's unique clam cuisine.

An excellent way to explore the entire town at your leisure is to stop by the Ipswich Visitor Center on Main Street to rent a self-guided audio tour. You can listen to local historian John Moss talk about more than fifty First Period homes, Ipswich artists past and present, agriculture and the environment. Skip around the sites in whatever order you'd like and just make sure you return the earpiece before the center closes at 5:00 pm. Call ahead (978-356-8540), as the center's hours are seasonal.

Alan Pearsall's seventeen-thousand-square-foot *History of Ipswich* mural is a focal point of the Ipswich Riverwalk. *Courtesy Alan Pearsall Art & Design.*

In 2006, the town opened a new riverwalk behind the Ebsco Publishing building on Estes Street. The entrance path is across from the Ipswich Visitor Center at the Hall-Haskell House, to the right of the Ipswich Artists Cooperative building at 59 South Main Street (part of what locals call the SoCho district, south of the Choate Bridge), and leads past fish ladders and a covered walkway to the vibrant Ipswich town history mural by artist Alan Pearsall. Wrap up a morning of strolling and sightseeing in Ipswich with a picnic lunch by the river and see how many historic town events you can pick out in the massive mural, which continues around the side of the Ebsco building. Author and orator Reverend John Wise is just one of the notable residents pictured there.

NATHANIEL WARD (1578–1652)

After an early career in law and studies throughout continental Europe, Nathaniel Ward was persuaded to enter the ministry in Prussia. Ten years later, he returned to his native England to become a rector in Essex, but his Puritan beliefs put him at odds with the leadership of the Church of England, and he immigrated to Massachusetts in 1634 to avoid excommunication.

Ward ministered in Ipswich for only two years before retiring in ill health, but not before delivering many impassioned speeches against toleration of differing Protestant sects. After leaving the ministry, he turned his attention to the governing of the new Massachusetts Bay Colony and drafted the first code of laws in New England, "The Body of Liberties." The document was adopted by the General Court of the Massachusetts Bay Company in 1641, while poet Anne Bradstreet's father, Thomas Dudley, was governor, and puts forth a set of Scripture-based values that was progressive compared to English common law at the time. These "Liberties" included the prohibition of compulsory military service except in defense of the country and the declaration that no man could be imprisoned without being charged. However, the "Liberties" also legalized slavery and imposed the death penalty for many infractions, listing belief in "any other god, but the lord god" and being a witch "that consulteth with a familiar spirit" as the two most egregious offenses. For his services in drafting these laws, Ward was granted six hundred acres of land in Pentucket, now Haverhill.

After drafting the "Liberties," Ward began work on *The Simple Cobler of Aggawam* (an earlier Native American name for the town that is now Ipswich). The punning subtitle, "Willing to help mend his Native Country, lamentably tattered, both in the upper-Leather and the Sole," hints at its place as the first work of satire in America. *The Simple Cobler* attacked the trend toward toleration, frivolity in women and the foppishness of men's contemporary dress. Published as a work of fiction under the pseudonym Theodore de la Guarde, the book nonetheless prompted colonial scholar Moses Coit Tyler to write:

> *Nathaniel Ward was a grumbler…Everything and everybody seemed to him to be going wrong. The times were out of joint… The difficulty between Nathaniel Ward and the age he lived in arose from the not uncommon fact that he shrank from the consequences of his own ideas. He was one of those unhappy persons with the brain of a radical and the temperament of a conservative.*[9]

As de la Guarde, Ward wrote, "My heart hath naturally detested foure things: The standing of the Apocrypha in the Bible; Forainers dwelling in my Countrey, to crowd out native Subjects into the corners of the Earth; Alchemized monies; [and] Tolerations of divers Religions." It is not difficult to imagine Ward as a colonial incarnation of contemporary political pundits railing against lenient immigration law and liberal politics. Later, his "cobler" takes up the mantle of "Herald of New-England" and, with tongue in cheek, grants these "forainers" and practitioners of "divers Religions" his full permission to stay far away from Aggawam:

[I] *proclaime to the world, in the name of our Colony, that all Familists, Antinomians, Anabaptists, and other Enthusiasts shall have free Liberty to keepe away from us, and such as will come to be gone as fast as they can, the sooner the better.*

PLACES TO SEE

Village Green Monument, Ipswich
A monument to Ward and others sits at the north end of Ipswich Village Green, diagonally across Route 133/County Road from the Whipple House.

ANNE BRADSTREET (C. 1612–1672)

Mirror of Her Age, Glory of her Sex, whose Heaven-born-Soul leaving its earthly Shrine, chose its native home, and was take to its Rest.
—from Reverend John Norton's eulogy for Anne Bradstreet, 1672

Unusually well educated for a woman of her time, the young Anne Dudley was doted on by her father Thomas, a steward to the Earl of Lincoln in England's eastern midlands and later governor of the Massachusetts Bay Colony. As a child, she composed poems for him, which he took delight in reading aloud with her.

When she was sixteen, she married Cambridge University graduate Simon Bradstreet, a colleague of her father's on the earl's estate. The young couple shared the strong Puritan beliefs with which Anne was raised and which continued to inform her thinking and writing.

In 1630, Simon was appointed secretary of the new Massachusetts Bay Company, and the Bradstreets, along with Anne's parents, became some of the first Puritan settlers to make the three-month journey to America on the ship *Arabella*. Life in the wilderness of this new colony was challenging, even for the heartiest souls, and by all accounts Anne was much stronger of intellect than of body. She had been a sickly child and battled constant fatigue throughout her life, along with bouts of smallpox and tuberculosis—all while raising eight children.

She and Simon originally settled in Salem but soon moved to Cambridge, to a cabin located in what is now Harvard Square. Simon's outspokenness and open ambition resulted in his being transferred from Cambridge to the colony's frontier, the wilderness of what is now Ipswich. Here, Anne wrote often during her husband's long periods of travel back to Boston and even a return trip to England.

As is expected for the age, Anne's poems explore Puritan values. However, she questions theology and draws less solace from strict doctrine than from what she calls God's "wondrous works": the simple miracles of sunrise and sunset, the changing of the seasons and nature's bounty. Her humility is not the result of blind adherence to theology, but rather a constant intellectual exploration of faith and the questioning of her own conscience. This independence of mind is all the more remarkable when one reads the calls against toleration made by family friend Nathaniel Ward, drafter of the "Massachusetts Body of Liberties."

Bradstreet never wrote for publication, and it was only because her brother-in-law brought some works back to England and had them published in 1650, possibly without her knowledge, as *The Tenth Muse Lately Sprung Up in America, By a Gentlewoman of Those Parts* that Anne Bradstreet is now known as the first female poet in America.

In *The Tenth Muse*, Bradstreet struggles with faith in the face of tragedy ("Verses upon the Burning of our House, July 18th, 1666"), thanks God for her recovery from illness ("For Deliverance from a Fever") and, touchingly even to contemporary audiences, expresses her love for her husband in poems such as "To My Dear and Loving Husband" and "A Letter to Her Husband, Absent upon Public Employment," in which she asks, "If two be one, as surely thou and I, / How stayest thou there, whilst I at Ipswich lie?" With Ipswich and Boston a good day's ride apart, and the threat of Indian attacks always looming over the lives of northern settlers, it is no wonder that Bradstreet often thought of and missed her husband.

Bradstreet's poems also display the extreme gratification of raising children and grandchildren. The following is taken from "In Reference to her Children":

> *I had eight birds hatcht in one nest,*
> *Four Cocks were there, and Hens the rest.*
> *I nurst them up with pain and care,*
> *No cost nor labour did I spare*
> *Till at the last they felt their wing,*
> *Mounted the Trees and learned to sing.*
> *Chief of the Brood then took his flight*
> *To Regions far and left me quite.*
> *My mournful chirps I after send*
> *Till he return, or I do end.*

And although she was by no means a reformer, Bradstreet's writing nonetheless displays moments in which she stands up for women's value in a humorous way. In these lines from her poem "In Honour of that High and Mighty Princess, Queen Elizabeth," she chides male readers that back in England just a few decades ago, their attitudes toward women would have offended their sovereign:

> *Now say, have women worth, or have they none*
> *Or had they some, but with our Queen is't gone?*
> *Nay, masculines, you have taxed us long;*
> *But she, though dead, will vindicate our wrong.*
> *Let such as say our sex is void of reason,*
> *Know 'tis a slander now, but once was treason.*

PLACES TO SEE

Waldo-Caldwell House, 25 High Street, Ipswich
A plaque in front of this private seventeenth-century house marks the site of the Bradstreets' homestead. This home was built after

Anne and Simon Bradstreet's Ipswich home stood on this spot more than three hundred years ago.

Ipswich Public Library.

1652 by Cornelius Waldo, an ancestor of author Ralph Waldo Emerson, and sold to John Caldwell only a few years later. Although Bradstreet didn't live in this exact home, High Street has many homes from the period in which she lived to inspire the imagination about what Ipswich may have been like during the poet's time. In fact, Ipswich has the highest concentration of extant First Period architecture in the country, and it is well worth a stroll to view the clapboard houses nestled in the shade of venerable oak trees.

Ipswich Library, 25 North Main Street, Ipswich
A few blocks from High Street is the Ipswich Library, originally built in 1868 with a comfortable 1995 addition. In the collection are rare editions of Bradstreet's work, as well as archival materials about the history of Ipswich. Call the reference librarian at 978-356-6648 or the Ipswich Historical Society at 978-356-2811 to make an appointment.

WILLIAM HUBBARD (1621–1704)

William Hubbard came to America as a child in 1630 as part of the Great Migration of Puritans. After graduating from Harvard in 1642, he became a member of the clergy and eventually led the Congregational church in Ipswich until a year before his death. Today, he is most remembered as the author of the 1677 volume *A Narrative of the Troubles with the Indians*, which was primarily an account of King Philip's War.

During Hubbard's tenure as pastor, Ipswich was on the outskirts of the Massachusetts Bay Colony, and attacks from Native American tribes were a daily fear of the English settlers, although the two groups had largely maintained an uneasy peace since John Winthrop Jr. led the first colonists into the area in 1633. In 1675, growing tensions came to a head when an Indian Christian convert and advisor to Wampanoag leader Metacomet (called King Philip by the English) was murdered. Three Wampanoag men were tried, convicted and hanged for the crime, but soon after, members of the allied Pokanoket tribe attacked the Rhode Island settlement of Swansea in retaliation for what they felt was an unjust trial. This episode ignited a two-year war that killed seven out of every eight Native Americans and almost half of the English settlers.

Hubbard's *Narrative* was a response to hellfire and brimstone preacher Increase Mather's 1676 book *Brief History of the Warr with the Indians*, which claimed that the war was God's punishment for declining morals among the Puritan settlers. Hubbard felt that the war was not a punishment, but a test of faith—not caused by Puritan failings, but by Native Americans' lack of faith in Christianity, aided by the greed of the Dutch and French traders who outfitted them. Historians Matthew Edney and Susan Cimburek write that Hubbard saw the war

> as a conflict between "Christian People" and their "Pagan Neighbours," between the English whom "the Father of Light…hath called…out from the dark places of the Earth" and the "Savages" who had yet to hear "the glad Tydings of Gospel Salvation" and who still inhabited a moral "Region of darkness."[10]

The *Narrative* was extremely popular in its time and was reprinted into the nineteenth century.

Thomas Franklin Waters (1851–1919)

Thomas Franklin Waters wrote more books about the people, places and events in Ipswich history than anyone has to date. From his home near the South Green, Waters served as the minister of Ipswich's South Congregational Church from 1879 until his sudden death in 1919. He founded the Ipswich Historical Society in 1890 and was instrumental in saving the 1677 Whipple House from destruction in 1898. His speeches, sermons, articles, monographs and books number in the dozens and include his monumental two-volume *Ipswich in the Massachusetts Bay Colony* (1905, 1917). The Ipswich Historical Society, on its website, quotes a colleague of Waters's who described him as a "persistent searcher after historical truth."

Waters was an early advocate for Native American rights and the truthful telling of their story in Essex County. In 1905, in the introduction to his history of Ipswich, he wrote:

> *The long, simple, uneventful ages of the wilderness period that ended when the white man came, must ever remain too dim, shadowy and ghost-like to be subjected to the historian's rigid method. But a fine sense of justice to the unnumbered generations of Indian men and women, that preceded our own ancestors in ownership…compels us not to ignore their unrecorded history, but to construct it as best we can.*

Places to See

96 County Road, Ipswich
Waters lived in this parsonage from 1879 to 1909 while he served as minister of the South Congregational Church. The house originally stood across the street; it is now closed to the public.

85 County Road, Ipswich
Waters lived here after he retired from the church.

Ed Emberley (b. 1931)

Occupying an entirely different corner of the North Shore's literary heritage is the prolific and popular children's book author and illustrator Ed Emberley. Author and illustrator of more than eighty books, including many collaborations with his wife, Barbara, Emberley studied at the Massachusetts College of Art and the Rhode Island School of Design in the 1950s and began publishing in 1961 with the notable *The Wing on a Flea*. The book *Drummer Hoff*, featuring text by Barbara and psychedelic woodcuts by Ed, received the Caldecott Medal for distinguished picture books in 1968.

A self-described "old grandpa kind of guy," his most popular works remain his series of how-to-draw books for children of all ages, which feature vibrant and whimsical step-by-step instructions for creating one's own imaginative illustrated world. He and his wife live in a 1690 saltbox house in Ipswich, where they continue to write and draw and run a private press called Bird in the Bush.

John Updike (b. 1932)

John Updike's genius is best excited by the lyric possibilities of tragic events that, failing to justify themselves as tragedy, turn unaccountably into comedies.
—Joyce Carol Oates

Born and raised outside of Lancaster, Pennsylvania, John Updike has lived in northeastern Massachusetts since 1957 and has written roughly one book per year over a career that spans more than half a century. He and his first wife, Mary Pennington, raised their four children in various homes in Ipswich, where Updike also worked in a small office in Caldwell's Block overlooking the Ipswich River. After he and Mary divorced, Updike lived in Boston, Georgetown and, finally, Beverly Farms. He has lived there since 1982 with his second wife, Martha, in a house set far back from the road among a landscape that Updike described in *Toward the End of Time* as "truly florid flora!"

John Updike.
Courtesy Random House.

Updike's work often concerns the trials of middle-aged men in suburbia, a subject that early reviewers sometimes found lacking in substance, but which many readers connected with. His first critical success, *Rabbit, Run* (1960), is set in the fictional Pennsylvania town of Brewer and concerns "Rabbit" Angstrom, a young husband and father in an unhappy marriage who pines for his days as a high school athlete. The novel's explicit sexuality worried Updike's publishers, but critics hailed it for its freshness. It introduced suburban adultery as an ongoing theme in Updike's work—a theme that has been picked up by many New England authors since, including Rick Moody in *The Ice Storm* (1994) and Tom Perotta in *Little Children* (2004).

In 1968, *Couples* gave Updike his commercial breakthrough. This controversial and amoral tale of failed and failing marriages put a decidedly bleaker spin on the 1960s' sexual revolution. The fictional New England town of Tarbox bears many resemblances to Ipswich, where the Updikes then lived. A review in *Time* magazine read:

> *Trapped in their cozy catacombs, the couples have made sex by turns their toy, their glue, their trauma, their therapy, their hope, their frustration, their revenge, their narcotics, their main line of communication and their sole and pitiable shield against*

the awareness of death. Adultery, says Updike, has become a kind of "imaginative quest" for successful hedonism that would enable man to enjoy an otherwise meaningless life.[11]

Rabbit Angstrom returned in four more volumes over the next fifty years, while Updike also explored other subjects such as complicated father-son relationships that mirror Greek mythology (*The Centaur*, 1963); political unrest in a fictitious African nation (*The Coup*, 1978); New England witches who seek revenge on the devil (*The Witches of Eastwick*, 1984, and *The Widows of Eastwick*, 2008); and teenage Muslim extremists in New Jersey (*Terrorist*, 2006).

To date, Updike has written more than sixty books and has received many of the literary world's highest honors. A two-time winner of the Pulitzer prize (for *Rabbit is Rich*, 1981, and *Rabbit at Rest*, 1990), he is also one of the few people to have received both the National Medal of Art and the National Medal for the Humanities.

Adam Frost, in *Literature Online*, hypothesizes about what Updike's ultimate literary legacy will be:

He will probably be remembered for providing his readers with a densely worded and astonishingly thorough catalogue of the objects, events and places that dominated late-twentieth-century life in middle America. He is also the finest realist in twentieth-century American letters: he describes what it is actually like to commit adultery in a small town in America in 1963, what it is like to bring up a son who disappoints you, what it feels like to sell cars for a living, what it feels like to find a long-lost daughter. Updike's finest novels are, in the best sense, windows into the past.[12]

PLACES TO SEE

The following homes are all private property, buildings where Updike lived and worked and on which he based some of his fictional locations.[13]

"Little Violet," Essex and Heartbreak Roads, Ipswich
The Updikes' first home in New England, this is where Updike began writing his first published novel, *The Poorhouse Fair*.

26 East Street, Ipswich
The pre-1687 Polly Dole House, a two-story clapboard structure, was the model for the Guerins' house in *Couples*. Updike lived here with his first wife and their four children from 1958 to 1970.

Caldwell Building, South Main Street, Ipswich
Updike rented a small office in this building at the foot of the Choate Bridge in 1961 and began writing here every morning, six days a week. As of 2008, the building was home to the Choate Bridge Pub, Chipper's River Café and various offices.

50 Labor-in-Vain Road, Ipswich
Having achieved significant critical and commercial success with *Rabbit, Run* and *Couples*, Updike moved his family to this large white house on the water in Ipswich, where he lived from 1970 until he and his wife separated in 1974. The Whitmans' house in *Couples* is based on 50 Labor-in-Vain Road.

ESSEX

The tiny coastal town of Essex, population just over three thousand, began life as Chebacco Parish, a part of Ipswich. Residents began agitating to split off from Ipswich in 1752, but Essex didn't become a separate town until 1819. One legend tells that Ipswich denied Essex townspeople the right to build a meetinghouse because that would confer a sense of autonomy to the town. The dictate supposedly read, "No man shall erect a meetinghouse," so a Mrs. Varney organized a group of very literal Chebacco Parish towns*women* to do the job.

Essex's Atlantic beach isn't accessible by land, but kayaking is a popular local activity. There are many places to easily enter the tidal Essex River for self-guided kayaking, and Essex River Basin Adventures offers guided sea kayaking tours to folks of all skill levels. A favorite summer evening activity for some locals is to get Chinese takeout from the Fortune Palace on 99 Main Street and kayak out to the shores of Bull or Cross Islands for a floating picnic.

Most tourists visit Essex for its seafood restaurants and its flourishing antiques trade. Over the past few decades, more and more shops have opened, concentrated along Martin and Main Streets, and now Essex boasts more antique shops per square mile than anywhere else in the country. In *New England Antiques Journal*, Noah Fleisher writes, "To an antiques treasure hunter...looking for

The Shingle-style Essex Town Hall and T.O.H.P. Burnham Library at 30 Martin Street, Essex.

that great little town that's been overlooked in recent years and that still contains a myriad of great buys on a variety of good antiques, Essex approaches buyers' nirvana."[14]

Essex's historic T.O.H.P. Burnham Library was built with funds bequeathed to the town by the affluent and eccentric used bookseller and publisher Thomas Oliver Hazard Perry Burnham. Dedicated in 1894, the library is the only example of Shingle-style civic architecture in the United States. It was added to the National Register of Historic Places in 2007.

Don't miss the legendary Woodman's Clams on 121 Main Street, where you can sample mouthwateringly greasy fried clams at the place where they were invented. If you're just passing through and need a refresher, the Village Market at the junction of Martin and Main Streets makes fresh sandwiches and has a large selection of massive homemade muffins that you can enjoy while watching local foot traffic at the post office right across the street.

REVEREND JOHN WISE (1652–1725)

An early activist against taxation without representation and a proponent of liberal church and civil government, Reverend John Wise was the American-born pastor of Chebacco Parish (now Essex) for more than forty years. In 1687, Massachusetts Bay Colony governor Edmund Andros briefly revoked Wise's position to punish the reverend for leading a town revolt against paying taxes that violated the colony's charter. The seeds of American democracy are found in this act, for which Ipswich's official town seal contains the phrase "The Birthplace of American Independence, 1687."

In 1710, Wise opposed famed preachers Increase and Cotton Mather when they suggested a new organizational hierarchy for colonial churches with a biting and quotably satirical pamphlet called *The Churches' Quarrel Espoused*, which seems to have quashed the Mathers' efforts. He later expanded on his belief in popular sovereignty—be it of churches or colonies—in his 1717 volume *Vindication of the Government of New England Churches*. In it, he reinforced his belief that a ruler's power comes from the people who elected him, not from divine right. Many scholars have noted similarities between Wise's *Vindication* and passages from the Declaration of Independence, positioning Wise as an early revolutionary in the fight for colonial rights. Hamilton Abert Long noted that Wise's *Vindication* "makes it clear that this 'age of philosophy' and this 'empire of reason' in America did not originate in the 1776 period but was in bud, if not in flower in remarkable degree, in Wise's day."[15]

An imagined portrait of Reverend John Wise in the *History of Ipswich* mural. *Courtesy Alan Pearsall Art & Design.*

Reverend John Wise's house stood here along present-day John Wise Avenue in Essex.

PLACES TO SEE

Ipswich Riverwalk, North Entrance (located at Faith's Garden pocket park across from the Memorial Common on South Main Street/Route 1A), Ipswich

John Wise is depicted as one of the pillars of Ipswich's early community in artist Alan Pearsall's Ipswich Riverwalk mural.

Former Home on Route 133, Essex

A section of Route 133 between Ipswich and Essex is named John Wise Avenue, and a plaque near mile marker 33.4 notes the site of his house, which is currently a private home. The house and marker can be found just past the White Elephant Antiques shop on the left as you head east into Essex.

Old Burying Ground (behind the Essex Shipbuilding Museum), 66 Main Street, Essex

Wise is buried in this historic graveyard, which was active from 1680 to 1852. His grave is at the center under a table-like stone.

Dana Story (1919–2005)

A historian and author, no one captured Essex's shipbuilding heritage like Dana Story. Descended from an old Essex shipbuilding family and a fifth-generation shipbuilder himself, Story devoted his life to telling and preserving the stories of "life, toil, and lore" in Essex shipyards and to "shed[ing] light on the ever-vanishing art of shipbuilding" that made Essex unrivaled in the world.

His books include *Growing Up in a Shipyard: Reminiscences of a Shipbuilding Life in Essex, Massachusetts* (1991) and *Frame Up! A Story of Essex, Its Shipyards and Its People* (reissued 2004). He also contributed significantly to the collection of the Essex Shipbuilding Museum, which stands on the grounds of Story's former shipyard.

In *Growing Up in a Shipyard*, Story wrote:

> *The existence of the shipyard seized my consciousness early on and, as soon as I was allowed away from home alone, I was drawn to climbing about the stagings and playing in and about the vessels. Days and days my friends and I would be there as soon as school let out. I quickly learned the nomenclature of a ship and its parts, and gained an appreciation of what the men were doing...Ah, how it all filled me with wonder. The methods and processes by which a wooden ship was built were indelibly etched upon my soul.*

Places to See

Essex Shipbuilding Museum, 66 Main Street, Essex
In addition to the shipbuilding museum adjacent to Dana Story's former shipyard, next to the historic *Evelina M. Goulart* schooner and the reproduction *Lewis H. Story* schooner, the museum also oversees a pre–Civil War hearse house and a nineteenth-century schoolhouse.

LYNN

The city of Lynn, the southernmost town on the North Shore, has struggled more than its neighbors to recover from the economic decline that followed the Great Depression. Its salty reputation made it the subject of an anonymous and largely undeserved singsong that begins, "Lynn, Lynn, city of sin," but this child's rhyme is by no means the only verse to have been written about the city. In 1880, local poet David Johnson hailed:

> *Favored of Fortune, lovely Lynn,*
> *Girt with her gem-emblazoned shore,*
> *Whose murmur soothes the city's din,*
> *We prize thee more and more.*

Today, Lynn is the focus of many efforts to revitalize its architecturally significant downtown and preserve the large historic homes that line Lynn Shore Drive. Spend an afternoon exploring the energy of this again up-and-coming city and seeing the sights that most inspired its poets.

Start at High Rock Tower, a stone observation tower with fantastic sweeping views of downtown, the peninsula of Nahant, Boston and the Atlantic Ocean. Lynn writers have memorialized this landmark for more than three centuries, from poet and minister Enoch Mudge

(1776–1850) and mayor Thomas Porter (1847–1927) to Elizabeth Merrill, whose 1900 poem "High Rock" was read at celebrations commemorating the city's fiftieth anniversary. Like David Johnson before her, she appreciates the blending of city noise and crashing waves. She writes:

> *Overlooking the town of Lynn,*
> *So far above that the city's din*
> *Mingles and blends with the heavy roar*
> *Of the breakers along the curving shore.*

From High Rock, to the left of the causeway that leads to Nahant is Egg Rock, formerly the site of a lighthouse and now a bird sanctuary. This, too, was a frequent subject for early Lynn poets and even makes a brief appearance in Winthrop, Massachusetts native Sylvia Plath's novel *The Bell Jar* when the protagonist dares her friend Cal to swim out to the rock from the beach.

In the opposite direction, one can see Lynn Woods Reservation, home to hiking and biking trails and a source of occasional intrigue during Lynn's early days. Alonzo Lewis was the city's most prominent civic poet, as well as the city's most comprehensive chronicler with his 1844 volume on Lynn history. With a nod to the area's seafaring history and pirate legends, he describes an event in May 1834, when "several persons destroyed the curious cave in the Dungeon Rock, under an imagination that they might obtain treasure."

From High Rock Park, head toward the shore through the city's historic Bank Block District along Exchange Street. Here, the LynnArts cultural center is a leader of the city's renaissance. Stop in to view exhibitions by local artists and check out the schedule for the Neal Rantoul Vault Theatre. The nearby Lynn Museum and Historical Society at 590 Washington Street is an excellent source for information about the city's history. Check to see if they are offering any walking tours on the day of your visit.

Today, Lynn has a significant Cambodian population, and on Chestnut Street one can see a contemporary *wat*, or temple, housed in an Italianate New England house.

Alonzo Lewis and the Lynn Poets

During his lifetime, Alonzo Lewis (1794–1861) was Lynn's leading intellectual, known as both the "Bard of Lynn" and the "Historian of Lynn." He began writing poetry as a young man for local periodicals, publishing his first volume of poems in 1823 and subsequent volumes in 1831 and 1834. Lewis also taught at the Lynn Academy, eventually becoming its principal. He edited a Lynn antislavery newspaper before William Lloyd Garrison launched the *Liberator* in Newburyport. Later, Lewis edited Garrison's newspaper, as well as the *Boston Traveller*. Lewis's definitive *History of Lynn* was first published in 1829 and remains one of the most important texts on the city's early history.

The following authors can also be grouped with the Lynn Poets—they are contemporaries of Lewis, as well as those who came before and since:

Enoch Mudge (1776–1850), a prominent Methodist minister, used poetry to preach. Mudge was the first minister at the Seaman's Bethel in New Bedford and the model for Father Mapple in Herman Melville's *Moby Dick*.

Darius Barry (1812–ca. 1880), primarily a maker of "morocco" or hand-tanned sheepskin, was also known for the lighthearted verse that he published in the *Lynn Transcript*.

Joseph Nye (1816–1901) was called the leading occasional poet of Essex County, a reference to the poems he wrote to commemorate important civic events. His book, *An Offering of Friendship*, was published in 1860, and his poems appeared frequently in Lynn newspapers through the turn of the century.

David Johnson (1824–1906) followed in the footsteps of his mentor Alonzo Lewis and became Lynn's leading intellectual in the second half of the nineteenth century. Like Lewis, Johnson was active in civic affairs; he wrote history (*Sketches of Lynn* published in 1880) and poetry (*Commemorative Poems* published in 1890).

Thomas Porter (1847–1927) was mayor of Lynn in 1907, as well as senator and state representative. His poetry was often published in Lynn and Boston newspapers and was collected in his 1906 book *City Songs and Country Carols*.

ANTOINETTE PURINTON, whose birth and death dates are unknown, was the only female poet of Lynn to publish a book of poetry in the nineteenth century.

LYDIA ESTES PINKHAM (1819–1883)

We'll drink a drink a drink
To Lily the Pink the Pink the Pink
The saviour of the human race
For she invented medicinal compound
Most efficacious in every case.

Mr. Frears
Had sticky-out ears
And it made him awful shy
And so they gave him medicinal compound
And now he's learning how to fly.
—*from a 1960s pop song by British pop group Scaffold*

One of the nation's first mail-order marketers was the shrewd businesswoman and Lynn native Lydia Estes Pinkham. The tenth of twelve children, Lydia Estes grew up in a politically active abolitionist family that counted Frederick Douglass as a friend. She founded a coed debating society at her high school, where she met her husband, Issac Pinkham. Though not exactly a leading literary light, her facility with written marketing launched one of the most well-known products of the nineteenth century and inspired many a media campaign in the years afterward.

In the mid-nineteenth century, when Lydia and Issac were raising their children, the medical profession was largely disorganized and mistrusted. Many homemakers brewed their own herbal concoctions in the kitchen, and Pinkham was no different. Her remedies were popular among her neighbors, and when Issac's real estate business fell on hard times, Lydia's son Daniel suggested that she begin accepting payment for a vegetable compound meant to treat menstrual and menopausal symptoms. The business took off—in part because Pinkham addressed the total void of reliable information about "women's concerns"—and moved to a factory on Western Avenue in Lynn. Lydia E. Pinkham's Vegetable Compound, promising to relieve "all those painful Complaints and Weaknesses so common to our best female population," was promoted through customer testimonials and letters from Lydia herself, whose face was on every bottle. Its nearly forty-proof alcohol content didn't hurt its popularity, especially when later generations of Pinkhams ran the company during Prohibition.

Lydia's Vegetable Compound remains one of the most well-known patent medicines, and scholars of women's medicine recognize Pinkham as one of the first people to speak straightforwardly about women's health issues. Although the medicine's efficacy may be in doubt, Pinkham's ability to use direct marketing, magazines and testimonials to her product's advantage mark her as one of the country's most successful early businesswomen.

PLACES TO VISIT

Pinkham Factory Building, 267–271 Western Avenue, Lynn
The site of the Pinkham Factory contains a number of small businesses and shops, including Pinkham Pottery and others that choose to honor the location's history. (The nearby Java's Brewin' coffee shop at the corner of Western Avenue and Chestnut Street offers baked goods, beverages and free WiFi access.)

Pine Grove Cemetery, 154 Boston Street, Lynn
Lydia Pinkham is buried in Lynn's Pine Grove Cemetery. The plot, marked by a tall stone with an urn finial, is within sight of the maintenance building.

NAHANT

The former resort town of Nahant, established on a sandy spit connected to Lynn by a narrow causeway, is known to history for the Boston luminaries who summered there. In his 1948 book *The Last Resorts*, Nahant native and humorist Cleveland Amory called Nahant "a stronghold of New England intellectuals" that has now become a "social ghost town." Thomas Appleton, the Boston artist and Henry Wadsworth Longfellow's brother-in-law, famously described Nahant as "cold roast Boston" because of its staid Boston Brahmin population. Today, Nahant is a quiet residential community of just over sixteen hundred households.

Henry Wadsworth Longfellow

(1807–1882)

Poet Henry Wadsworth Longfellow, his wife Fanny and their children spent many summers in Nahant, first in 1850 as guests at the Jonathan Johnson house (Longfellow describes it as a "long, low house in the village"). It was here in 1854 that he began the famous book-length poem *The Song of Hiawatha*. By 1856, the Longfellows were spending summers at the Mountford Cottage. The poet writes in a letter to his friend the statesman Charles Sumner that the cottage "boasts one of the finest situations in Nahant...From this little room in the attic I look over the broad Atlantic, with nothing between me and England."[16] At Mountford, Longfellow worked on *A New England Tragedy*, his three-part work on Christianity in the Apostolic, Middle and Modern Ages.

Longfellow's journals are full of the sights and sounds of Nahant. (In his journal from July 12, 1854, he writes: "Last summer's life resumed, as if after a sleep. Carriages drive by, cocks crow, hens cackle, the dust flies, the sea gleams in the distance.") But he often looked forward to leaving at the end of the summer as much as he looked forward to visiting in the spring. In a journal entry from 1860, he confesses of the difficulty of getting work done at Nahant: "How lazy the seaside is! If only one had no conscience!"[17]

Beginning in 1857, he rented the Wetmore Cottage on Nahant's eastern side, which he and his brother-in-law Thomas Appleton purchased in 1860 after the owner's death. For the next twenty-five years, until his death in 1882, he spent his summers at the brown cottage by the willows. Sadly, the Wetmore Cottage was lost to fire in 1896, fourteen years after the poet's death. An article in the *Boston Transcript* declares, "The fire in Wednesday's wind and dust on the lovely headland will be talked of regretfully overseas, also, as it would not have been if all of the newer and finer Summer homes at Nahant had been swept away."[18]

PLACES TO SEE

339 Nahant Road, Nahant
When Longfellow stayed at the Jonathan Johnson house, it was located across the street from the present-day 339 Nahant Road, on the site of what is now the Richland store. Number 339 was an early Nahant summer cottage, and many of its eight outbuildings

have since been torn down or converted to separate residences.

Mountford House, 3 Swallows Cave Road, Nahant
One of the Longfellows' summer homes was along this road at the southernmost tip of Nahant's eastern branch. It remains an impressive private home with one of Nahant's best ocean views.

Former Site of the Wetmore Cottage, Willow Road (near Cliff Street), Nahant
The home that Longfellow and his brother-in-law purchased in 1860 stood near the beach that parallels Vernon Street in this tree-filled corner of eastern Nahant.

Marine Science Center, 430 Nahant Road, Nahant
The Nahant Hotel once stood on this site before burning down in 1861. Longfellow stayed at the hotel often, including one visit in the summer of 1847, when he addressed a letter to Charles Sumner from the dormer window at room number 75.

MARBLEHEAD

Founded by settlers who left nearby Salem and its Puritan leaders, Marblehead sits on land once governed by the Naumkeag tribe, from whom a group of selectmen bought the land for sixteen pounds in 1684. The town's access to fishing banks led to the development of a thriving commercial fishing industry, although that began to wane by the mid-1800s. Today, a number of commercial vessels still sail from Marblehead, but the harbor has become more of a home for pleasure craft and international races, leading to its nickname as the yachting capital of the world.

The Spirit of '76 bookstore at the corner of Pleasant and School Streets is the hub for many area reading groups, and the staff there can recommend all kinds of books by local authors and about Marblehead: *Leviathan: The History of Whaling in America*, by Eric Jay Dolan, made nonfiction bestseller lists in 2007. And debut author Katherine Howe's witch trial tale, *The Physick Book of Deliverance Dane*, made a splash when the manuscript was the focus of a bidding war among publishers. Although author Ben Sherwood isn't from Marblehead, his 2004 novel *The Death and Life of Charlie St. Cloud* is set here, and the Spirit of '76 booksellers describe it as an accurate depiction of the town, with local spots like Maddie's Sail Loft restaurant making appearances. Just steps from the bookstore is the Atomic Café and the Marblehead Little Theatre on School Street.

Marblehead Neck and the sailboat-dotted Marblehead Harbor. © *Doc Searls*.

The café is a popular downtown coffee shop, and the theatre in an old firehouse shows movies on Fridays in the summer.

ASHLEY BOWEN (1728–1813)

The first American sailor known to write his own autobiography, Ashley Bowen began his seafaring career at the age of eleven. He was apprenticed to Captain Peter Hall from age thirteen to seventeen and describes severe beatings and harsh treatment, but this didn't dim his love for sailing. For almost twenty years, he made his living on the sea, including joining the British navy and being held prisoner by the French during the Seven Years' War that ended France's rule as a colonial power. After marrying his first wife and starting a family, he chose to remain onshore as a ship rigger in Marblehead.

A witness to significant historical events, including the British conquest of Canada and the American Revolution, Bowen's eighteenth-century interpretation of events is informed by his deeply religious beliefs and his suspicion of Yankee patriotism. Drawing on original journals owned by the Marblehead Museum and Historical Society, historian Daniel Vickers edited and published *The Autobiography of Ashley Bowen, 1728–1813* in 2006.

PLACES TO SEE

Marblehead Museum and Historical Society, 170 Washington Street, Marblehead
The museum houses Bowen's original journals. Call ahead to make an appointment to view his writings and watercolor drawings.

AMESBURY

Where the North Shore meets the Merrimack Valley, just two miles from the New Hampshire border, lies the town of Amesbury. With its mixture of the pastoral and the industrial, Amesbury encompasses both the grittier history of Merrimack River mill towns and the agrarian roots that make so many North Shore towns so picturesque.

Its manufacturing history includes being the home of the first mechanized nail-making factory, as well as a time when the Merrimac Hat Factory's production was higher than any other milliner in the nation. The Powwow River's ninety-foot falls powered downtown textile mills, which marked Amesbury's transition from a Federal-period farming and shipbuilding community to a nineteenth-century mill economy. From the 1850s through the 1920s, Amesbury was the center of the American carriage-making industry. A 1999 mural on Main Street by Jon P. Mooers depicts residents in their horse-drawn carriages in front of the Powwow River mills. This transition from agriculture to industry happened during the course of poet John Greenleaf Whittier's lifetime and accounts, in part, for the fact that his later work tended toward nostalgic reflections on a simpler past.

Today, Amesbury is a successful example of a city that has used its industrial architecture to revitalize its downtown, by transforming

The Powwow River falls behind Amesbury's Mad River Tavern.

mill buildings and factories into offices, stores and restaurants that surround landscaped pockets of public green space. The Mill District Walking Tour that begins at Market Square is a self-guided walk that leads through some of these transformed places, with plaques that fill visitors in on the history but don't detract from the restored architecture, new parks and gardens and historic views.

Among the many places to stop for a drink or a meal in Amesbury is the Mad River Tavern, which features a small outdoor patio overlooking the rolling Powwow River just below the falls and the revitalized Market Square complex. Across a small public amphitheatre from the tavern is the much-lauded Flatbread Baking Company, a high-ceilinged brick room whose centerpiece is a large wood-fired oven where the staff turns out perfectly baked pizzas and flatbreads using distinct organic ingredients. You'll want to leave room for their sundaes made with homemade baked goods and rich vanilla or pumpkin ice cream.

A few buildings to the south of the carriage mural and Market Square, another Mooers mural pays homage to one of Amesbury's most famous residents, the poet and abolitionist John Greenleaf Whittier, who spent much of his adult life in a house on Friend Street.

In the winter, northern New England's waterways ice up enough that bald eagles come as far south as the Merrimack River to fish, and Deer Island offers a promising view of these winter visitors.

John Greenleaf Whittier (1807–1892)

I am not one of the master singers and don't pose as one. By the grace of God, I am only what I am and don't wish to pass for more.
—*John Greenleaf Whittier*[19]

Poet, politician and abolitionist John Greenleaf Whittier was born in Haverhill but spent his adult years in Amesbury. After he and his brother sold and split the profits from their family's farm in 1836, he purchased a home on Friend Street and moved there with his mother, sisters and aunt.

After getting involved with an antislavery rally in Amesbury in 1833, Whittier felt personally connected to the struggle. He began writing and lobbying for abolitionist causes and eventually became the editor of the local *Anti-Slavery Reporter*. So vocal was his opposition to slavery that he drew violent detractors when he spoke, dodging rotten eggs in Newburyport and narrowly escaping when the Philadelphia offices of the Anti-Slavery Society were burned by an angry mob. His first authorized volume of poetry was published in 1838 while he was living in Philadelphia and editing the *Pennsylvania Freeman*.

Whittier's own political aspirations began to cool around 1850, after he had persuaded the outspoken antislavery advocate

John Greenleaf Whittier, 1885. *Courtesy Library of Congress, LC-USZ6-277.*

Charles Sumner to embark on a successful Senate campaign. His poetry became less about reform and more about reflection, although he remained involved in abolitionist causes until the end of the Civil War and Emancipation.

His "winter idyll" *Snow-Bound,* a book-length reminiscence of a childhood blizzard that his family waited out together in Haverhill, was published in 1866, surprising Whittier with its success and allowing him to live comfortably for the rest of his life. The next year, according to the Whittier Homestead's website, the publication of *The Tent on the Beach, and Other Poems* "makes explicit his decision to 'lay aside grave themes, and idly turn / The leaves of memory's sketch-book.'"

Whittier died in 1872 while visiting friends in New Hampshire and is buried in the family plot near his sisters and mother.

Places to See

Whittier House, 86 Friend Street, Amesbury
Whittier moved to the white clapboard home with his mother, sister and aunt in 1836, when the family's homestead in nearby Haverhill became too difficult to manage on his own. The Amesbury property is maintained by the Whittier Home Association, which purchased the house and ground in the early twentieth century. It remains virtually unchanged since Whittier lived there, and a live-in caretaker also serves as curator, giving the house a sense of life, as

The John Greenleaf Whittier House in Amesbury.

if the Whittier family has just briefly left the home in a neighbor's care. Even the poet's overcoat lies across the bed in the guest room, as if he had decided not to pack it after all.

A handmade bedcover is one of the interesting domestic touches at the Amesbury house. A white embroidered bedspread in his sister Eliza's room reads "Whittier A.D. 1837." Among the other artifacts on display is a marble bust of Whittier, original pages of his manuscripts and, for those unaffected by a touch of the macabre, the poet's death mask.

J. Denis Robinson, writing for *Seacoast NH*, says of Whittier's study, "English lit majors should not enter this room without a defibrillator,"[20] and indeed, it is rare to be allowed such intimate access to an author's workspace, still filled with priceless volumes of his own work and that of colleagues who inspired him. It was in this room that Whittier composed his most lasting work, the poem *Snow-Bound*. Despite the overwhelming literary history, one of the most charming details of the room is a tiny peephole at the top of the door where, the guide tells us, Whittier's pet finch flew in and out.

Friends Meeting House, 120 Friend Street, Amesbury
Whittier was on the building committee when this Quaker meetinghouse was constructed in 1850. His usual spot at meetings is still marked with a plaque reading "Whittier's Bench."

Amesbury Public Library, 149 Main Street, Amesbury
The Amesbury Public Library, a 1900 Romanesque revival building only a few blocks from the meetinghouse on Main Street, includes a wide selection of books by and about Whittier, including a number of first editions from 1870 and earlier. A librarian can help you find these historic volumes.

Captain's Well, 220 Main Street (adjacent to Amesbury Middle School), Amesbury
Another nearby Whittier landmark is the Captain's Well on Main Street adjacent to the middle school. The well was dug by Amesbury native Captain Valentine Bagley to fulfill a promise that he had made to God while he was shipwrecked off the Arabian coast. Bagley swore that if he returned to New England alive, he would build a well so that no man ever had to suffer from thirst as he had. Bagley's story had become local legend by the time of Whittier's childhood, and when the captain died in 1839, the people of Amesbury and neighboring Newburyport gathered to celebrate his life. Harriet Spofford delivered a speech that inspired her friend Whittier to imagine this defining moment in Bagley's life and faith:

> *"Why dig you here?!" Asked the passerby;*
> *"Is there gold or silver the road so nigh?"*
>
> *"No, friend," he answered: "but under this sod*
> *In the blessed water, the wine of God."*

After he succeeds in reaching water, he spends his days sitting by the well and watching travelers come and go:

Amesbury Public Library.

The Captain's Well on School Street in Amesbury.

And when a wayfarer weary and hot,
Kept to the mid road, pausing not

For the well's refreshing, he shook his head;
"He don't know the value of water," he said;

"Had he prayed for a drop, as I have done,
In the desert circle of sand and sun,

"He would drink and rest, and go home to tell
That God's best gift is the wayside well!"

The mossy, stone-walled rest stop still features a public fountain and the foundations of the very well dug by the captain. Bagley is buried in Amesbury's Union Cemetery, not far from Whittier himself.

Union Cemetery, Route 110 (entrance between Main and Highland Streets), Amesbury
Heading west on Route 110 (also called John Greenleaf Whittier Highway), turn left at the first cemetery entrance directly across from J.E. Moghan Memorials. Less than one hundred yards from the road, a tall pine tree on the left bears a faded green sign that points the way to Whittier's grave. A few paces down is a sign for "Whittier Path," from which you will see "Here Lies Whittier" just above the poet's simple grave. The Union Cemetery is adjacent to both the Barlett Cemetery and the St. Joseph Cemetery, so be sure to enter via the first road on the left or you'll need to walk around a low stone wall to reach the site. Whittier's grave is near one of the oldest sections of the cemetery, where weatherworn and broken headstones mark the resting places of early settlers from the first half of the eighteenth century.

SALISBURY

Sitting at the farthest northeast corner of Massachusetts, the small town of Salisbury is known as a summer beach community, with fewer than eight thousand year-round residents. As of the 2000 census, nearly 90 percent of Salisbury was open space—farms, beaches and marshlands. The ship *Jennie Carter* wrecked off the coast in 1894, and its remains can still be seen at low tide. Eighteenth-century author Hannah Webster Foster was born here, and twentieth-century poet Edna St. Vincent Millay lived here briefly as a child.

PLACES TO SEE

Ring's Island is a colonial fishing village at the end of Ferry Road that faces Newburyport across the Merrimack River. The 1680 Jonathan Dole House on Third Street was a childhood home of author Edna St. Vincent Millay.[21]

NEWBURYPORT

Looking at Newburyport's well-maintained central district, the historic residential neighborhoods and the crowds that flock to the waterfront and surrounding restaurants and shops all summer long, it would be difficult to guess that the city has weathered a catastrophic fire and two significant periods of economic hardship in its 250-year history.

Home to Pawtucket Native Americans before the arrival of the Puritans, the area was settled as part of Newbury in 1630. Located at the trout-rich south bank of the Merrimack River where it runs to the Atlantic Ocean, inland Newbury developed an agrarian economy, while the port was home to fishermen and traders. Shortly before the American Revolution in 1764, the port was so thickly settled that it was able to break off from Newbury and establish itself as the separate, newly christened town of Newburyport. The immense Federal mansions built during this period of prosperity sit atop hilly lawns, shaded by massive, two-hundred-year-old oak trees.

The first few decades of the nineteenth century brought challenges and a swift downturn. A disastrous fire in 1811 leveled the downtown, and the economic embargoes imposed during the War of 1812 threw Newburyport's economy into a tailspin. However, like many neighboring communities, the Industrial Revolution

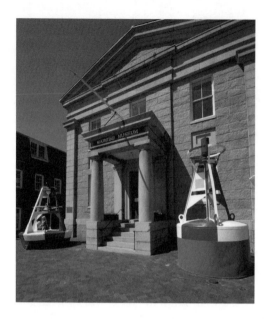

Newburyport Custom
House Museum.

arrived with new opportunities and steam-powered mills that drew power from the Merrimack and provided new jobs. The fire codes established in the wake of 1811's tragedy guided the design of the historic mid-nineteenth-century brick buildings that now give the downtown its unique charm.

Along with much of northeastern Massachusetts, particularly towns that were able to harness the power of the Merrimack for mill power, Newburyport struggled into the early twentieth century, when the loss of industrial and manufacturing jobs throughout the region left the brick mills empty and looming over an increasingly downtrodden downtown landscape.

Newburyport has been more successful than many of its neighbors in holding on to its past while revitalizing for the future. The urban renewal movement of the 1970s was particularly successful, and that decade saw the construction of the charming waterfront park and boardwalk. Today, the park hosts concerts, outdoor movie screenings and festivals. Independent retail shops and restaurants slowly filled in the former factory structures along Water and State Streets. A nineteenth-century tannery has become a small shopping mall that includes a bakery, boutiques and the popular Jabberwocky Bookshop. At the corner of the tannery mall on Water Street, don't miss the upscale Joppa's Market, which stocks artisanal cheeses, fresh sandwiches, tempting baked goods and imported candies to snack on while you stroll. The shops at the tannery are just across the street from the Custom House Maritime Museum, a compact collection of art and artifacts from Newburyport's time as a major commercial seaport.

Many visitors concentrate on this vibrant waterfront area, but the few blocks of residential neighborhoods between Water and High Streets make for a wonderful walk through New England history. Many historic homes have been spectacularly maintained and still display the shingles, siding and ornamental woodwork that early seafarers employed to craft a house that would display their success and wealth.

In her biography of novelist John Marquand, Millicent Bell describes his trolley car ride from his aunt's home at Curzon Mill to Newburyport High School at the corner of Green Street:

> *The trolley car would come jangling and swaying along its uneven track, and after he got on, it would go along Storey Avenue, slanting west through fields and woods, finally intersecting with High Street, down which it turned in the direction of Bartlet Mall at the center of Newburyport... Along this street lived a good many of the oldest families in town, and some, though not all, of the richest. A few of the houses shone crisply fresh-painted and stood on smooth rises of lawn; others were graying behind overgrown gardens. Yet to live on High Street in any of these houses was to live along a ridge of social as well as physical elevation above others.*[22]

The newly inaugurated Newburyport Literary Festival, which honored Andre Dubus II in its first year, celebrates local authors and promotes a love of literature through programs in middle schools, public lectures and readings, as well as celebrations of the continuing love for the written word on the North Shore and beyond. The weekend festival takes places every April and has featured local authors Andre Dubus III, Ed Emberley, crime novelist and doctor Keith Ablow, music journalist Peter Guralnick and many, many more writers who make their homes on the North Shore.

WILLIAM LLOYD GARRISON (1805–1879)

It was the glory of this man that he could stand alone with the truth, and calmly await the result.
—Frederick Douglass, at a Washington, D.C. memorial for William Lloyd Garrison

A passionate and outspoken advocate of abolition, William Lloyd Garrison did not receive the privilege of an upper-class education. Growing up in Newburyport as the son of a merchant sailor, Garrison and his family, like many of their neighbors, fell on hard times in the early years of the nineteenth century, when the Embargo Act severely limited American vessels' ability to dock in foreign ports. Garrison's father abandoned the family when William was only three; the boy had to sell candy to earn money for the family, and they relied on the charity of Newburyport's wealthy.

The young Garrison's career path began with his teenage apprenticeship at the *Newburyport Herald*, where he was an assistant type compositor. While still a young man, he began to publish articles in the paper, and when he turned twenty-one he purchased a small newspaper of his own, the *Free Press*.

The first major step in his career as a reformer came in 1829, when he moved to Baltimore to work with Benjamin Lundy on the Quaker newspaper the *Genius of Universal Emancipation*. Lundy advocated a gradual retreat from slavery, while Garrison came to favor an immediate and total emancipation of all slaves. The newspaper made room for both viewpoints, although it was

William Lloyd Garrison, no date given. *Courtesy Library of Congress, LC-USZ62-10320.*

Garrison who bore the brunt of proslavery attacks on the paper. He was even briefly jailed for libel after publishing the names of slave trade profiteers in the *Genius*'s "Black List" column.

Feeling the need to more fully promote his absolutist antislavery position, and now with the publishing and editorial experience to support it, Garrison parted ways on good terms with Lundy and left the *Genius* to return to Newburyport. It was here in 1831 that he founded one of the most influential abolitionist newspapers of the era, the *Liberator*. Unafraid to speak out strongly in favor of his beliefs, the paper's inaugural editorial included this proclamation:

> *I do not wish to think, or speak, or write, with moderation…I am in earnest—I will not equivocate—I will not excuse—I will not retreat a single inch—AND I WILL BE HEARD. The apathy of the people is enough to make every statue leap from its pedestal, and to hasten the resurrection of the dead.*

Benjamin Lundy was not the first fellow reformer with whom Garrison had parted ways over ideological differences about reaching their common goal. He had earlier left the American Colonization Society when he believed that their goal of offering freed slaves a home in Western Africa masked a desire to strengthen what would then remain of institutionalized slavery. Later in life, his support of feminist leaders such as Lucy Stone and Lucretia Mott caused a rift in his own American Anti-Slavery Society (AAS), of which a majority of members supported barring women from joining. His falling out with Frederick Douglass over Garrison's anti-Constitutional views—he believed that the document supported slavery—lasted decades, and the two did not reconcile until after the Civil War.

From its founding in 1831 through the Emancipation Proclamation in 1865, the *Liberator* grew from four hundred subscribers to more than three thousand and served as a major public voice of dissent. Garrison's impassioned arguments against slavery retain their zeal even 150 years later. His editorial in the paper's inaugural issue contained the following wish and set the tone for his writing and oratory: "Let southern oppressors tremble—let their secret abettors tremble—let their northern apologists tremble—let all the enemies of the persecuted blacks tremble."[23] John Greenleaf Whittier, whom Garrison had met when Whittier's sister sent the poet's work to Garrison's Newburyport *Free Press*, was a lifelong contributor. Garrison traveled throughout the country speaking out against slavery and received numerous death threats because of it. A lynch mob chased him through the streets of Boston after he gave a speech to the Boston Female Anti-Slavery Society. Garrison spent the night in jail for his own safety and was obliged to leave town for a few weeks until the situation cooled down.

After the Civil War ended, Garrison declared his life's work to be complete. He folded the *Liberator* and stepped down as head of the American Anti-Slavery Society. Although both he and the leaders of the AAS saw the need to continue fighting for the rights of blacks, Garrison felt that this cause would be better served by new organizations, new leadership and newly refocused goals. As happened so often in his life, this refusal to compromise led to hard feelings between Garrison and those who chose to remain with the AAS. Now in his sixties, he continued to speak out for temperance and civil rights for blacks, and he became involved with the American Women's Suffrage Association.

He spent his final years caring for his ailing wife, and after her death, he lived in New York City with a daughter and her family. He died in 1879 and is buried in Boston's historic Forest Hills Cemetery.

Pioneers of Freedom *carte de visite*, including portraits of Charles Sumner, Henry Ward Beecher and William Lloyd Garrison, circa 1866. *Courtesy of the Library of Congress, LC-USZ62-111195.*

Garrison Inn on Main Street, Newburyport, 1929. *Photo by Leon Abdalian, courtesy Boston Public Library.*

PLACES TO SEE

Statue in Brown Square (corner of Green and Pleasant Streets), Newburyport
The small green space of Brown Square has monuments to Newburyport's war veterans, as well as a towering statue of Garrison. Author John Marquand, attending high school in Newburyport in the 1900s, tells of passing the statue every day on the trolley to school. Directly across from the statue is the 1790s Garrison Inn. Once shipbuilder Moses Brown's home, it has been a hotel since 1880.

Garrison's Birthplace, 3–5 School Street, Newburyport
The clapboard structure in which Garrison was born is now a twin private home next to the historic Second Presbyterian Church and across from the small Atwood Park.

William Lloyd Garrison was born in this modest clapboard house in 1805.

HARRIET PRESCOTT SPOFFORD (1835–1921)

Spofford always finds the vermilion and azure threads woven into the duns and grays of the New England life and women she knew so well.
—Thelma Shinn Richard[24]

Born in Calais, Maine, in 1835, Harriet Prescott Spofford began writing as a way to help support her family. Before she was born, her father sought to reverse his failing fortunes in the West, but he returned from the journey as an invalid and had difficulty keeping his boardinghouse business afloat. The family relocated to Newburyport, where Harriet was able to attend the Putnam Free School and Pinkerton Academy despite her family's lack of resources. Raised in a family headed by women, and with a clear talent for writing, Spofford's creativity was encouraged from an

Harriet Prescott Spofford, no date given. *Courtesy Library of Congress, LC-DIG-ggbain-04716.*

early age, and she developed into one of her era's most widely published short story authors.

In 1859, her story about a diamond theft, "In a Cellar," was published in the *Atlantic Monthly*, but only after Spofford was able to convince publisher James Russell Lowell that it was indeed her work and not a translation from the French. Lowell was skeptical that a story of such high quality had come his way from an unpublished author, and a woman no less. From that time on, she regularly published short fiction in that magazine and others. Much of her output was driven by a need to contribute to her family's income, and her body of work includes pieces in which she clearly opted for commercial viability over laboriously worked craftsmanship, although she was indisputably a master of the gothic romance and spun chilling and rich ghost stories.

At age thirty, she married the lawyer Richard Spofford and moved to Deer Island, a small parcel of land between Newburyport's

Chain Bridge and southern Amesbury. Her financial prospects now much more stable than in her youth, she nevertheless continued to publish as prolifically as ever.

Her 1830 story "Circumstance" is the only one likely to be found in current anthologies of the era. Loosely based on a real event in her great-grandmother's history, it is the story of a woman who is followed and trapped overnight by a demonic creature. At first calling for her husband's help, the protagonist is ultimately able to protect herself through the ordeal by singing until her husband is able to find her.

> *Slow clarion cries now wound from the distance as the cocks caught the intelligence of day and re-echoed it faintly from farm to farm,—sleepy sentinels of night, sounding the foe's invasion, and translating that dim intuition to ringing notes of warning. Still she chanted on. A remote crash of brushwood told of some other beast on his depredations, or some night-belated traveller groping his way through the narrow path. Still she chanted on. The far, faint echoes of the chanticleers died into distance,—the crashing of the branches grew nearer. No wild beast that, but a man's step,—a man's form in the moonlight, stalwart and strong,—on one arm slept a little child, in the other hand he held his gun. Still she chanted on.*

Thelma Shinn Richard writes in the *Heath Anthology of American Literature*:

> *Spofford's gift is to treat the sensational or implicitly "romantic" event realistically: a very real wife and mother draws on the art of her life—the hymns and lullabies and folk tunes she has sung—to placate a wild beast and defend herself against death.*

The story both spooked and impressed Emily Dickinson, who was reportedly a great fan of Spofford's fertile imagination. She was quoted in the *Atlantic Monthly* as stating, "I read Miss Prescott's 'Circumstance,' but it followed me in the dark, so I avoided her."[25] About the story "The Amber Gods," she said, "It is the only thing I ever read in my life that I didn't think I could have imagined myself."[26] Spofford died at her home in 1921 at the age of eighty-six.

PLACES TO SEE

Spofford Home on Deer Island
The chain bridge is a Newburyport landmark that links the city to Deer Island in the Merrimack River. First built in 1792, a sign details the 225-foot suspension bridge's many renovations, rededications and expansions. Deer Island's only structure and Spofford's former home was originally a tavern catering to Boston–New Hampshire travelers making use of the new bridge. It was converted to a home decades before Spofford and her husband moved there in 1865, when she was thirty. Spofford lived in this home for the rest of her life and died there at age eighty-six in 1921.

Her sister, Mary Newmarch Prescott, the author of many children's stories and the volume *Matt's Follies*, lived here briefly with the Spoffords. After returning from a year of traveling in Europe, Mary fell ill and died at the home in 1888.

A parking area immediately across from the house at the foot of the chain bridge has access to Deer Island's hiking trails and fishing holes, but it allows only an obstructed view of the Spoffords' former home, which remains a private residence.

Oak Hill Cemetery, Newburyport
Spofford's grave at Oak Hill Cemetery is a little tricky to find, but it is not far from the gatehouse at the main entrance. Heading southeast on State Street, turn right onto Brown Street (called Greenleaf Street on the left side of State) and pass a handful of houses on the way to the large gated entrance. Drive just a few hundred yards, passing a rutted dirt path on your left, to where the main loop through the cemetery splits left and right. At this "intersection," you should see a large marker for the Anthony family on the right, a dark stone marking the Green-Pingree family

Harriet Spofford's gravestone in a quiet, wooded section of the historic Oak Hill Cemetery.

plot on the left and, just past a dirt turnoff on the right, some stones marking the Ashby family. Pull in and park at this turnoff on the right—it's the first place where a car could reasonably make a right turn—and walk away from the road, toward the tree line and pond. A line of about ten headstones, three rows down the hill from the main road and the Ashby stones, marks the resting places of members of the Prescott and Spofford families. Harriet Prescott Spofford's stone is near the middle and bears an inscription paying tribute to her skill as "a poetess."

Steps and pathways in the older sections of the cemetery are in various states of repair, and the terrain slopes down toward the Oak Hill pond to the west, so if you plan to explore, wear comfortable sneakers. The pastoral landscaping, ancient trees, sometimes overgrown bushes and many headstones commissioned from talented artists to honor loved ones passed are well worth an hour's quiet stroll around the grounds.

JOHN MARQUAND (1893–1960)

His are not the best books I've ever read, but they are among the books I love most, and the neglect into which they have fallen is a literary outrage.
—*Jonathan Yardley in the* Washington Post[27]

John Marquand knew well the trials and tribulations of life as a member of an American blue-blooded family and skewered the dilemmas of class with sharp satire. His ancestors were successful Federal-era merchants in Newburyport who lost everything during the fire of 1811. John grew up visiting his relatives at Curzon's Mill in Newburyport and hearing tales of the Marquand and Curzon (on his mother's side) families' past glories. His paternal grandfather had been an extremely successful businessman, but supporting an extended family stretched his resources so that after he died, the money ran out quickly without his business acumen behind it. In the meantime, though, the family lived in high style in Rye, a suburb of New York City, complete with automobiles, private schools and household staff. After John's father's rocky business prospects finally failed during the stock market crash of 1907 and his grandfather's largesse was long gone, the young man was sent to live with his eccentric aunts at Curzon's Mill while attending Newburyport High School.

It was there that Marquand learned that Newburyport was not only made up of the wealthy old families of High Street. His classmates included the children of office workers, clerks and immigrant laborers, and he praised this experience of education without class barriers throughout his life. Biographer Millicent Bell writes that the students "strolled as far as the statue of William Lloyd Garrison, that poor Newburyport boy whose fame was a reminder that not all history had been made by High Street."[28]

With an admirable pedigree—albeit one generation removed—but no current prospects, he managed to win a scholarship to Harvard in 1911. This was during the university's peak as a bastion of privilege,

Illustration accompanying John Marquand's story "The Jamaica Road" in the *Saturday Evening Post*, July 4, 1925. *Courtesy Library of Congress.*

when private dormitories outfitted with servant's quarters were maintained for the wealthiest students along a stretch of Cambridge's Mount Auburn Street then known as the Gold Coast. The cliques and clubs that were a result of these rarefied living situations were critical to Harvard social life, and Marquand, merely a public school graduate without a name, was considered "unclubbable." Interested in journalism, he tried but failed to find a place with the *Harvard Crimson* newspaper, but he became closely involved with the school's renowned humor magazine, the *Harvard Lampoon.*

His first book was published in 1925 about Newburyport eccentric "Lord" Timothy Dexter. Other books skewering New England's high society followed, including the pseudo-memoir *The Late George Apley*, which prompted Upton Sinclair to write:

> *I started to read it and it appeared to me to be an exact and very detailed picture of a Boston aristocrat, and as I am not especially interested in this type, I began to wonder why you had sent it to me. But finally I began to catch what I thought was a twinkle in the author's eye...One can never be sure about Boston, and I hope I am not mistaken in my idea that the author*

is kidding the Boston idea. It is very subtle and clever, and I am not sure that Boston will get it.[29]

Not all of Boston society did get the joke, but Marquand had the last laugh when Mr. Apley won him a Pulitzer Prize in 1938. In addition to his satirical work, he also published the bestselling "Mr. Moto" spy novels, which were made into a series of films starring Peter Lorre in the 1930s. Despite his social outcast beginnings, his first wife was Christina Sedgwick, niece of the *Atlantic Monthly* editor Ellery Sedgwick, and through his second wife he became linked to the Rockefeller family.

He remains notable for the quips offered by his characters ("I know a fellow who's as broke as the Ten Commandments") and by the author himself ("I wrote the scenes by using the same apprehensive imagination that occurs in the morning before an afternoon's appointment with my dentist").

PLACES TO SEE

Sawyer's Hill Burying Ground and Maudslay State Park, 74 Curzon Mill Road, Newburyport

Marquand is buried in the Sawyer's Hill Burying Ground, near Maudslay State Park on Curzon Mill Road. After a walk through the cemetery, where other graves date to the seventeenth century, spend some time in the park, located on 480 acres of the former estate of Frederick S. Moseley, a Boston broker from the turn of the twentieth century. The park boasts one of the largest naturally occurring stands of mountain laurel in Massachusetts. From 1849 to 1870, the Laurel Grounds overlooking the Merrimack were the scene of an annual literary party, with such guests as the poet John Greenleaf Whittier.[30] Ornamental trees and masses of azaleas and rhododendrons bloom in May and June. Outdoor concerts and performances, as well as theatre-in-the-round, take place on the grounds in the summer months.

Rhina Espaillat (b. 1932)

The word, in any and all of its guises, is worth celebrating, because no other human invention has done more to give us access to the world we live in. The word allows us to name, define, describe, and preserve what we encounter of the world; the word allows us to bridge time by studying the past through its writings and leaving our own record for the future; the word allows us to communicate across borders, and—thanks to translation—even across the borders between languages. The word, finally, allows us to distill, analyze, embellish, and invent human experience to create literature.
—Rhina Espaillat

Born in the Dominican Republic, Rhina Espaillat moved with her family to the United States when she was just seven years old. She writes in both English and Spanish and works to bring bilingual poetry readings to audiences in Boston and on the North Shore—especially high school students in Lawrence and Newburyport. In her poem "Bilingual/Bilingüe," she talks about her father's determination that the family speak Spanish at home and leave English at the door. Not as fluent as his daughter, Espaillat writes that perhaps her father feared that her ease with this new tongue would separate them:

> *My father liked them separate, one there*
> *one here (allá y aquí), as if aware*
>
> *that words might cut in two his daughter's heart*
> *(el corazón) and lock the alien part*
>
> *to what he was—his memory, his name*
> *(su nombre)—with a key he could not claim.*

Deeply involved in the North Shore poetry community, she coordinates the monthly Powwow River Poets workshop and reading. Espaillat was the 2008 honoree at the Newburyport Literary Festival.

PLACES TO SEE

Newburyport Art Association, 65 Water Street, Newburyport
Powwow River Poets hosts monthly poetry readings at the Newburyport Art Association's gallery. A featured visiting poet and a Powwow member both read from their recent work, and an open mic session follows, during which visitors can sign up to share their own words with the crowd. Visit www.newburyportart.org for schedules and information.

ANDRE DUBUS III (B. 1959)

It's an amazingly rich community. In Newburyport, they had a fundraiser for the library. They invited all the published writers…thirty showed up. I had no idea. Just in that twenty-mile radius.
—*Andre Dubus III*[31]

Andre Dubus III first gained national recognition for his writing with his 1999 novel *The House of Sand and Fog*. The book was shortlisted for the National Book Award, chosen for Oprah's Book Club and made into a 2003 movie starring Ben Kingsley and Jennifer Connelly—all propelling Dubus into the world of literary celebrity, although he describes himself as being removed from the Boston-centered literary scene.

His father, Andre Dubus II, was a celebrated short story author, and the younger Dubus briefly studied at Bradford College, where his father taught. Despite his father's reputation, he didn't want to

Andre Dubus III. *Courtesy Random House.*

follow in his footsteps, and he didn't consider pursuing a writer's life until his early twenties. "I always felt sorry for those guys, you'd see those trucks 'Ralph & Sons.'…I never wanted to be [a writer]. That's the last thing I wanted to be."[32] But his talent for fiction, ignited by a bit of romantic jealousy when a woman he was dating admired a story another man had written, turned into real inspiration, and Dubus began pursuing the craft in earnest. While writing *The House of Sand and Fog*—working construction, teaching writing at three different colleges and helping to raise three young children—he wrote in his car, parked near a cemetery, just to find a quiet place to work.

Dubus continues to live in Newburyport with his wife and children. He published his fourth book, *The Garden of Last Days*, in 2008.

PEABODY

In the seventeenth century, Peabody was a part of Salem. In the eighteenth century, it was part of Danvers. And in 1868, it finally became its own town, named for the philanthropist George Peabody, who was born there in 1795. Giles and Martha Corey and John Proctor, all victims of the 1692 witch hysteria, lived in what is now Peabody. Where farming and the leather-tanning industry once flourished, the North Shore Mall is now the biggest contributor to the town's economy.

HANNAH WEBSTER FOSTER (1758–1840) AND ELIZA WHITMAN (1752–1788)

Author Hannah Webster Foster was born in Salisbury to a wealthy merchant, and although few biographical details about her exist, her writing shows evidence that she was unusually well-educated for an eighteenth-century woman. She began writing political articles in the 1770s for Boston newspapers before marrying Reverend John Foster in 1785. After giving birth to six children, she wrote

The Coquette, a bestseller about a contemporary Peabody scandal, and *The Boarding School* before returning to newspaper writing. She died in 1840 in Montreal, where she had moved to be near her daughters.

The Coquette was a bestseller in its time, although its scandalous subject meant that it was only published anonymously until after Foster's death. The epistolary novel tells the story of Eliza Wharton, based on the real-life Eliza Whitman, a distant cousin of Foster's. Whitman was a respected poet who died in Peabody from complications following the stillborn birth of her illegitimate child. Her story spread throughout the region as gossips speculated about who the father could be and how Whitman had allowed herself to be so debased. In 1798, William Hill Brown suggested that one of the reasons for Whitman's downfall was due to her being a reader of novels, which had turned her "vain and coquettish" and given her impossibly high standards for romance.[33]

In *The Coquette,* Foster offers a rebuttal to these moral lessons and examines how women could follow their hearts yet remain accepted members of society. She quotes Whitman's own poetry in her preface:

> *O youth beloved! what pangs my breast has borne*
> *To find thee false, ungrateful, and forsworn!*
> *A shade and darkness o'er my prospect spreads,*
> *The damps of night and death's eternal shades.*
> *The scorpion's sting, by disappointment brought,*
> *And all the horrors of despairing thought,*
> *Sad as they are, I might, perhaps, endure,*
> *And bear with patience what admits no cure.*
> *But here my bosom is to madness moved;*
> *I suffer by the wrongs of him I loved.*

In the following excerpt, the character Wharton's fictionalized paramour Peter Sanford has just brought his disgraced and pregnant lover to a secluded home for her "lying in" and reports to a friend on her depressed state and his inability to make amends for it.

> *It would hurt even my delicacy, little as you may think me to possess, to have a wife whom I know to be seducible. And on this account I cannot be positive that even Eliza would retain my love.*

Sanford later admits, "To her I lay not the principal blame, as in like cases I do the sex in general. My finesse was too well planned for detection." But his own success in seducing Eliza is what prevents him from considering her a trustworthy wife. Far from blaming her fictional Eliza Wharton—or lofty ideas gleaned from idle reading—for her own downfall, Foster ascribes her misery in large part to men's manipulation and hypocrisy. In doing so, she makes articulate claims for women's independence and challenges Brown's assertion that novels are dangerous for women by turning the novel into a vehicle for moral criticism and social change.

PLACES TO SEE

Old South/Trask Cemetery, Main Street, Peabody
Eliza Whitman, the woman whose tragic story inspired Foster's *The Coquette*, is buried here. Her original gravestone still stands, although it has been chipped at by more than two centuries of souvenir hunters. In 2004, the Peabody Historical Commission and the Peabody Institute Library erected a new stone next to it.

Lexington Monument (corner of Main Street and Washington Street), Peabody
This monument to Peabody's Revolutionary War soldiers stands near the former site of the Bell Tavern, where Whitman died. The tavern was torn down in the nineteenth century, but its stone doorstep remains. (According to historian Charles Knowles Bolton, writing in the 1912 volume *The Elizabeth Whitman Mystery at the Old Bell Tavern in Danvers*, Whitman was attended in her final moments by a neighbor, Mrs. Very, an ancestor of the poet Jones Very.)[34]

DANVERS

The town of Danvers was originally part of Salem Village, and it was here that most of those accused of witchcraft in 1692 actually lived. During the Revolution, Danvers was home to tidal mills, brick-making kilns and, later, tanneries and shoemaking. Much of the earliest architecture still survives, including the First Period Putnam House and Rebecca Nurse Homestead, both with ties to the witch trials.

John Greenleaf Whittier had a winter home here called Oak Knoll, and prominent abolitionist Alfred Fellows entertained many of his famous compatriots, including Harriet Beecher Stowe and William Lloyd Garrison, at his home at 48 Elm Street (now a private house).

PLACES TO SEE

Site of Oak Knoll (near where Summer Street intersects Greenleaf Drive), Danvers
Whittier's winter retreat is no longer standing—it was destroyed by fire in 1858 and razed to make way for a mid-century housing development in 1959. Oak Knoll was his cousin's home and served as Whittier's "county seat" from 1875 until his death in 1892. This was

the height of his fame, and the stream of admirers at his Amesbury home made working there difficult. The pastoral landscape and relative anonymity of Danvers was a welcome respite.

Biographer William Sloane Kennedy, writing just three years after Whittier's death, becomes a touch poetic when describing the land:

> *There are trees and trees at Oak Knoll,—smooth chestnuts with cool foliage, maples, birches, and purple beech. Add to the picture the rural accessories of bee-haunted clover-fields, apple and pear orchards, and beds of tempting strawberries.*[35]

Peabody Institute Library of Danvers, 15 Sylvan Street, Danvers
This magnificent Georgian revival building was dedicated in 1892, the gift of philanthropist George Peabody, for whom the neighboring town is named. The Danvers Archival Center at the library contains a wealth of materials related to the witch trials, as well as photographs, documents and manuscripts by and about John Greenleaf Whittier. The ghost of an old man is rumored to have been seen shushing patrons in the library's reading room.

BEVERLY

Across the Essex Bridge from Salem, the town of Beverly offers a glimpse of New England history where it meets the contemporary energy of the Montserrat College of Art and funky eateries like the Atomic Café on Cabot Street.

Beverly was officially incorporated when settlers from Salem split over religious differences in 1668. Few houses remain from this early era, but the 1679 John Balch house still stands and is open to the public. The city bills itself as the birthplace of the American navy (although Marblehead next door also claims the title) because the first commissioned warship—the schooner *Hannah*—sailed from Beverly Harbor in 1775. The industrial age brought the massive United Shoe Machinery Corporation, which occupied a building more than a quarter-mile long in what is now the Cummings Center on Route 62. A number of locations are named for hometown poet Lucy Larcom, including Larcom Avenue just north of Beverly Common and the Larcom Theatre on Wallis Street.

Beverly had its share of wealthy Bostonian summer residents during the mid-nineteenth century, when the North Shore was known as Boston's Gold Coast. Some of the era's huge "cottages" can be seen along Hale Street/Route 127 in Beverly and Prides Crossing. The village of Beverly Farms to the northwest on the way to Manchester also had its share of notable summer

Beverly Farms Branch Library.

residents—most prominent was Oliver Wendell Holmes Sr., whom historian Joe Garland calls "the peppery little anatomist and poet."[36] His name, along with that of Lucy Larcom and current Beverly Farms resident John Updike, adorns the new addition to the Beverly Farms Branch Library. Take a walk from the library around Hale Street, past the firehouse to West Street and grab a gourmet sandwich or fresh organic produce at the Fruitful Basket or treat yourself to an elegant lunch at the Cygnet.

OLIVER WENDELL HOLMES (1809–1894)

Poet, essayist, novelist, humorist, scientist, ripe scholar, and wise philosopher, if Dr. Holmes does not, at the present time, hold in popular estimation the first place in American literature, his rare versatility is the cause. In view of the inimitable prose writer, we forget the poet;...laugh

over his wit and humor, until, to use his own words,
"We suspect the azure blossom that unfolds upon a shoot,
As if Wisdom's old potato could not flourish at its root;"
and perhaps the next page melts us into tears.
—*John Greenleaf Whittier in honor of Oliver Wendell Holmes's*
seventy-fifth birthday, August 1884

Although trained as a physician, Oliver Wendell Holmes achieved lasting fame as one of the country's most notable nineteenth-century poets. A descendant of the poet Anne Bradstreet, Holmes attended Phillips Academy in Andover, Harvard College and the École de Médecine in Paris. He published on medical topics throughout his life, but he came to prominence as a poet in 1830, when the frigate USS *Constitution* was to be broken up for scrap. His commemorative poem "Old Ironsides" stirred patriotic sentiment to save the ship that had weathered Revolutionary battles. The final stanza suggests that it would be more honorable for the ship to sink to a watery grave than to become scrap wood. Thanks in part to Holmes's

That "peppery little anatomist and poet" Oliver Wendell Holmes Sr., circa 1889. *Courtesy Library of Congress, LC-DIG-pga-00067.*

poem, the *Constitution* was saved from being decommissioned and remains to this day in the Charlestown Navy Yard as the country's oldest commissioned warship.

> *Oh, better that her shattered bulk*
> *Should sink beneath the wave;*
> *Her thunders shook the mighty deep,*
> *And there should be her grave;*
> *Nail to the mast her holy flag,*
> *Set every threadbare sail,*
> *And give her to the god of storms,*
> *The lightning and the gale!*

Holmes and his literary colleagues Henry Wadsworth Longfellow, John Greenleaf Whittier, William Cullen Bryant and James Russell Lowell were known as the Fireside Poets, in part because their traditionally styled verses were easy to memorize and share around the hearth. Their work had strong moral themes and dealt with mythology and legend, as well as American politics.

Places to See

Beverly Farms Library, 24 Vine Street, Beverly Farms
Holmes had a summer house on Hale Street in Beverly Farms, where he is commemorated on the façade of the new library addition on Vine Street. In the library, one can sit at a roll-top desk that was once owned by the author and donated to the library by his son, Supreme Court Justice Oliver Wendell Holmes Jr. A model of Cyrus Dallin's Native American sculpture *Appeal to the Great Spirit* overlooks a massive carved wooden chair, both also owned by the Holmes family and given to the library to honor Oliver Wendell Holmes Sr.'s fondness for this high-ceilinged and light-filled branch of the Beverly Library system.

LUCY LARCOM (1824–1893)

I can conceive of no greater damper upon one's poetic attempts than the cold water of criticism. It is from heart to heart, from friend to friend, that I write; and I find in that the highest inspiration to do my best…One gives out life in writing; and nothing but life in return—life enlarged and filled—gives any true satisfaction.
—Lucy Larcom, letter to S.T. Pickard, 1880[37]

Although Larcom is most closely associated with the life of early Lowell mill girls, her autobiography about growing up in Beverly Farms, *A New England Girlhood, Outlined from Memory*, is her most lasting literary contribution. Written when she was sixty-five and the Industrial Revolution had already transformed much of the North Shore's rural landscape, it is filled with nostalgia for simpler times and vistas that disappeared long before the turn of the twentieth century.

In the title poem of her 1880 volume *Wild Roses of Cape Ann*, Larcom shows a touch of regret at the "strangers" who have bought up local land in Beverly. But she expresses a similar sentiment to that offered by Joe Garland in Gloucester more than a century later—outsiders may discover the town's charms and bring significant change, but the land truly belongs to those who have worked it and honored it for generations.

> *Strangers have found that landscape's beauty out,*
> *And hold its deeds and titles. But the waves*
> *That wash the quiet shores of Beverly,*
> *The winds that gossip with the waves, the sky*
> *That immemorially blends, listening*
> *Have reminiscences that still assert*
> *Inalienable claims from those who won,*
> *By sweat of their own brows, this heritage.*

PLACES TO SEE

Beverly Central Cemetery (entrances on Hale Street between Dane and Lothrop Streets), Beverly

Larcom is buried in this neighborhood cemetery under a simple stone with a quill, signifying her place as a woman of letters.

ELLERY SEDGWICK (1872–1960)

He was the editor of almost the best-known American magazine, and a very good editor at that...He met all the right people and knew all the right gossip. He has a fund of good stories, some of them really new, and almost all of them well told.
—Harold J. Laski[38]

Ellery Sedgwick took over the *Atlantic Monthly* in 1908, nearly fifty years after its founding by a group of Boston literary lights that included Oliver Wendell Holmes, James Russell Lowell, Harriet Beecher Stowe, John Greenleaf Whittier, Ralph Waldo Emerson and Henry Wadsworth Longfellow. Over his thirty-year tenure as editor, he increased the publication's circulation tenfold and brought many now canonical authors to American audiences for the first time. It was during Sedgwick's time at the head of the magazine that the *Atlantic Monthly* purchased "Fifty Grand" from the as-yet-unpublished author Ernest Hemingway. But Sedgwick's eye for new talent wasn't always so keen. His first encounter with Robert Frost came when he rejected the poet's submissions with a note that read, "We are sorry that we have no place in the *Atlantic Monthly* for your vigorous verse."[39] In 1946, Sedgwick published *The Happy Profession*, a volume of anecdotes and reminiscences peppered with references to many literary lights and social climbers of his era.

PLACES TO SEE

Long Hill, Essex Street, Beverly

For a true escape at any time of the year, visit Sedgwick's retreat at Long Hill, his family's vacation home. Surrounded by one hundred acres of woodland, meadows and apple orchards in Beverly, Long Hill is a gardener's dream. Sedgwick's first wife, Mabel Cabot, was an accomplished horticulturalist and established a garden that features distinct rooms and personalities, from a formal croquet lawn to a rustic fenced-in cutting garden. From the first mild days of spring through the final leaves of autumn, the garden at Long Hill is a constantly changing oasis surrounding the Sedgwicks' 1925 Federal-style house, a re-creation of an 1812 mansion in Charleston, South Carolina, that had been abandoned.

Picnicking is permitted at Long Hill, so spread a blanket in the shade of the house and imagine yourself at one of the grand garden parties that must have taken place on these premises in

Ellery Sedgwick's country retreat at Long Hill.

the 1930s and '40s. In mid-spring, massive stands of azaleas and rhododendrons sweep away any lingering memories of winter weather. Wisteria vines drip with blossoms around the front portico, attracting bumblebees with their sweet scent. The unusual handkerchief tree, a native Chinese variety, produces its distinct blooms in late May. These translucent single "petals"—actually a leaf-like structure called a bract—are what give the tree its name.

Two miles of easy hiking trails surround the property and offer great chances to view woodland ecology up close. Frogs croak in broad vernal pools and ferns grow thick on the forest floor. Pack plenty of insect repellent, though, and consider wearing long pants—the mosquitoes love the woods, too. Long Hill has been managed by the Trustees of Reservations since Sedgwick's second wife, Marjorie Russell, passed away in 1978. The Trustees hold occasional plant sales and maintain an extensive gardening reference library at the house, which is open to the public on weekdays from 9:00 a.m. to 5:00 p.m.

HAMILTON

The bedroom community of Hamilton was once a part of Ipswich known as the Hamlet and was named for President Alexander Hamilton when it was incorporated in 1793. Today, its many large estates and the open fields of the Myopia Hunt Club (founded during author Mary Abigail Dodge's lifetime) give Hamilton its wide-open and rural character. Hamilton's most famous native son is the World War II general George S. Patton Jr., for whom Patton Park, across the street from Myopia Hunt Club, is named.

MARY ABIGAIL DODGE (1833–1896)

Hamilton-born Mary Abigail Dodge graduated from the Ipswich Female Seminary in 1850 and taught there until 1854. At the age of twenty-four, she accepted a position in Hartford to teach English, simultaneously contributing to local newspapers, including the antislavery journal *National Era*, under her pen name Gail Hamilton. The *Era*'s publisher, Dr. Gamaliel Bailey, was so taken with Dodge's writing that he invited her to Washington, D.C., as his children's governess. She stayed for two years, publishing political articles and establishing herself as a writer of national stature. Dodge returned to Hamilton in 1860 to care for her ill mother.

From 1865 to 1867, she edited the magazine *Our Young Folks* with Lucy Larcom of Beverly. Her books include *Country Living and Country Thinking* (1862), *A New Atmosphere* (1865), *Woman's Wrongs: A Counter-irritant* (1868) and *The Battle of the Books* (1870). While Dodge did not support women's suffrage, thinking it was not the most effective way for women to influence change, she spent most of her life trying to improve the status of women through her writing. "The nursery has no business to be the mother's chrysalis," she wrote. "God never intended her to wind herself up into a cocoon. If he had, he would have made her a caterpillar."

PLACES TO SEE

8 Gail Avenue, Hamilton
Dodge's former home remains a private residence.

SALEM

Salem's history is inextricably linked to the events of the Witch Hysteria of 1692, during which more than 150 people were accused of witchcraft, and fourteen men and five women were put to death for the crime.

Not surprisingly, this dark era in America's early history is fruitful ground for authors of fiction and nonfiction alike. From classic work like Arthur Miller's *The Crucible* to contemporary fare such as *The Physick Book of Deliverance Dane* by Katherine Howe, "Witch City" turns up as location and inspiration in literature again and again.

Contemporary Wiccan culture, Halloween revels and the serious history of a unique and tragic episode in American history all add flavor to downtown Salem. Author Brunonia Barry describes the town in the 1990s:

> *Hearses full of tourists drive slowly along the city streets. Convenience stores sell crystals and love potions. Costumed Frankensteins hand out fliers to everyone who happens by. Although Salem has been vigorously trying to change its Witch City image, the whole town's economy is tied to its dark history, and any change at all is a hard sell. Even the police cars in Salem sport the Witch City logo.*[40]

The city isn't trying to lose its witch history too quickly, though. In 2005, it erected a bronze statue of television witch Elizabeth Montgomery, star of *Bewitched*, in Lappin Park at the corner of Washington Street and Essex Mall, drawing controversy from residents.

But this large North Shore city has much more to offer than just ghost stories and pop culture witches. Many of the country's most prosperous eighteenth-century merchant ship captains called Salem home, and the town's many Federal-style mansions were built with the spoils of the Far East trade. Lucy Larcom writes in *A New England Girlhood* how, in Salem and neighboring Beverly:

> *Men talked about a voyage to Calcutta, or Hong Kong…as if it were not much more than going to the next village…Women of well-to-do families had Canton crape* [sic] *shawls and Smyrna silks and Turk satins for Sabbath-day wear.*[41]

The three-masted *Friendship* in Salem Harbor is a 1998 reconstruction of a 1797 East Indiaman built in Salem by Enos Briggs. The original *Friendship* made fifteen voyages to China, Java, Sumatra, Madras, London, Hamburg, Archangel, St. Petersburg and other European ports before it was captured by the British during the War of 1812. Its successor is the largest wooden Coast Guard–certified vessel built in New England in more than a century and is open for tours that leave from the Salem Maritime NHS Orientation Center at 160 Derby Street.

Federal-period architect and woodcarver Samuel McIntire was a major influence on the historical district that now bears his name. Dedicated in 1981, the district is the city's largest and contains 407 houses roughly bordered by Broad, Flint, Pickering and Fleet Streets. Essex Heritage offers a walking tour of the district that takes in both humble cottages and captain's mansions. Download a copy of the self-guided tour at essexheritage.org.

The Peabody Essex Museum, America's oldest operating museum, opened in 1799 as a place to house and display the many treasures that families like the Saltonstalls and Crowninshields had

The three-masted East Indiaman *Friendship* in Salem Harbor. © *Paul Keleher*.

collected from the West Indies, China, Africa and Russia. In 2003, the museum underwent a major renovation and now presents art and culture from New England and around the world. The museum campus features numerous parks, period gardens and twenty-four historic properties, including Yin Yu Tang, a two-hundred-year-old house that is the only example of Chinese domestic architecture on display in the United States.

Like many of its neighboring cities, Salem is home to a growing Caribbean and Central and South American immigrant population that is adding a new layer to the town's international culture. Today, the area of town known as the Port is home to a vibrant Dominican community with many first- and second-generation immigrant families. The next generation's artists and authors are likely to reflect this bicultural and bilingual change in the city's fabric.

SAMUEL SEWALL (1652–1730)

The diary of Samuel Sewall not only narrates the homely activities of Boston in the evening of the theocracy…but it unconsciously reveals the transformation of the English Puritan to the New England Yankee.
—*Vernon Parrington*[42]

Massachusetts jurist Samuel Sewall is best known for his role in the Salem witch trials, where he participated in convicting twenty-six people of the felony of witchcraft. He was the only magistrate involved in the trials to later apologize for his role in the tragedy. His 1700 essay "The Selling of Joseph" is the first antislavery pamphlet published in America and places him as one of the country's first abolitionists. In it he writes, "Forasmuch as Liberty is in real value next unto Life: None ought to part with it themselves, or deprive others of it, but upon most mature Consideration."

His involvement in the witch trials and his public expression of regret years later are the subject of two recent biographies,

Judge Sewall's Apology: The Salem Witch Trials and the Forming of an American Conscience by Richard Francis (2005) and *Salem Witch Judge: The Life and Repentance of Samuel Sewall* by Eve Laplante (2008). Before these studies brought Sewall back onto the radar of popular nonfiction, he was best known for his copious diaries, which were published by the Massachusetts Historical Society 150 years after his death and form an important record of colonial New England.

The *Norton Anthology of English Literature* writes of an interlude in the judge's life that was historically insignificant, yet memorable to scholars of early American letters:

> *Sewall's pursuit of the hand of the widow Katherine Winthrop has provided most readers of American literature with needed comic relief in the drama of Puritan salvation. There is something very satisfying in looking over the shoulder of the distinguished jurist subjecting his pride and reputation to the whims of courtship and adopting the role of petitioner.*

Of course, Sewall's life and career were far more distinguished and complex than his love-struck moments would lead us to believe. The unguarded revelations in his diary make it clear that it was written for his eyes only, and not for posterity, and may therefore present a more accurate version of colonial life than diaries kept by his contemporaries. Notably, considering his later refutation of the witch hysteria, his diaries contain little comment on that entire period of his career.

REVEREND WILLIAM BENTLEY (1759–1819)

Like Samuel Sewall one hundred years earlier, the Reverend William Bentley's most lasting contribution are the diaries he kept during his decades as a minister, scholar and columnist in Salem.

He was the Unitarian minister of Salem's East Church for more than three decades and turned down political appointments offered by Thomas Jefferson simply because he preferred life among his parishioners and community.

His personal library was one of the largest in the country, containing more than four thousand volumes, and he frequently gave young learners access to it and encouraged them in their studies. Mathematician Nathaniel Bowditch was just one of the many recipients of his support. Bentley could converse in seven languages and read twenty-one. He was a frequent contributor to the *Salem Gazette* and *Register*, and his sermons were always topics of conversation for the following week. His preaching emphasized the importance of good deeds and kindness, and he often invited ministers from other denominations to speak at the East Church. He believed in living modestly and boarded with the Crowninshield family for the last thirty years of his life. He was a founder of the East India Marine Society—which became the Peabody Essex Museum—and he donated his massive library to various schools, including Tufts and Harvard Universities and Allegheny College.

He was also well liked because he was a good-humored gossip. In February 1790, he shares this anecdote, representative of the kind of local dirt he enjoyed hearing, in his diary:

> *An anecdote of Bishop Seabury from Rev'd Andrew Eliot of Fairfield. He was applied to by a number of Episcopalians in an inland town to administer confirmation and baptism. As they had no house of worship, their neighbors the dissenters respectfully offered...the use of the Congregational meeting house to the Bishop. With sovereign disdain he replied, I HAVE NEVER, & I NEVER INTEND TO OFFICIATE IN AN UNCONSECRATED HOUSE. The disgust of his partizans [sic] was so great that they renounced Episcopacy & joined the dissenters.*[43]

PLACES TO SEE

Crowninshield-Bentley House, Peabody Essex Museum, Salem
This Georgian-style house was built for sea captain John Crowninshield in the late 1720s, when it originally stood curbside at 106 Essex Street. It was given to the Peabody Essex Museum by the Hawthorne Inn and moved to PEM's campus in 1959. Today it is open for seasonal tours with museum admission. Although the house is a fine example of Georgian colonial style, its most important historical aspect is that Reverend Bentley lived here from 1791 to 1819.

Harmony Grove Cemetery (bordered by Mount Vernon, Tremont and Grove Streets and Harmony Grove Road), Salem
Bentley is buried in this historic cemetery bounded by stone walls in northern Salem.

NATHANIEL BOWDITCH (1773–1838)

A profound influence on mathematics and navigation, Salem native Nathaniel Bowditch quite literally wrote *the* book on navigation. His major work, the 1802 *New American Practical Navigator*, is still the foremost and most wide-ranging reference work on the subject. He was also America's first insurance actuary, a distinction that is perhaps not glamorous, but which set a course for the insurance industry as it exists today. Almost entirely self-taught, Bowditch's story is the kind of classic up-by-the-bootstraps tale that permeates Federal New England history.

Nathaniel's father, Habakkuk, was a cooper, and at the age of ten the boy had to leave school to work in his father's shop, but he stayed only two years before being indentured as a bookkeeping apprentice to a ship's chandler. Chandlers are responsible for tracking the supplies needed to outfit a ship and restocking at port. For the nine years that he lived in the home of his master,

Nathaniel Bowditch pictured in a full-size bronze statue at Mount Auburn Cemetery, Cambridge.

Bowditch was surrounded by logbooks and accounts and had use of the man's library. Bowditch was able to teach himself Latin, French, algebra and calculus in the evenings and during his rare free time when no ship was docking in Salem. By the time he was eighteen, this young man with little formal education was already so well versed in mathematics that he was corresponding with Harvard professors to point out errors in their published work.

Bowditch also benefitted from the support of William Bentley, a popular, benevolent and extremely well-learned Unitarian preacher, author and diarist who was well respected throughout Salem. Bowditch's access to Bentley's massive library—he was a ravenous reader who housed a collection of more than four thousand volumes—as well as the preacher's endorsement of the young man's talents, opened many doors.

Bowditch's indentureship ended when he turned twenty-one, and he soon after made his first sea voyage, this time as a ship's clerk. He would make four more trips, the final one as captain and part owner, and throughout these voyages he worked on updates to what was then the preeminent navigational text of its time, John Hamilton Moore's *New Practical Navigator*. By the time the 1802 edition of this work was to be published, Bowditch had corrected more than eight thousand errors and expanded upon the work so thoroughly that it had become an entirely new text. Newburyport publisher Edmund Blunt decided to release Bowditch's work as the first edition of a new book, and the *New American Practical Navigator* was born.

Bowditch, having limited formal education himself and having spent time with sailors who may have been excellent seamen but lacked "book learning," understood the necessity of writing in a voice that anyone could understand. Salem historian Jim McAllister writes, "It became, along with 'a Bible, a chest of clothes and mother's blessing,' an essential part of every seaman's gear." When the book's copyright expired in 1866, the United States government bought the rights and reissued it as a government publication, required onboard any commissioned U.S. Navy ship. Its clear-cut language and substantial information on navigation, maritime law and ship terminology remain relevant more than two hundred years after its initial publication.

The success of the *Navigator* brought an honorary master's degree from Harvard and allowed Bowditch to settle his family in a comfortable home in Salem. He became president of the Essex Fire and Marine Insurance Company, which prospered under his direction for two decades. During this time, he continued to study and publish on mathematics and astronomy and fielded offers to be the chair of the mathematics departments at Harvard, the University of Virginia and the United States Military Academy. Yet this man who had stopped attending school at age ten turned them all down and chose to remain in Salem with Essex Fire and Marine.

In 1823, he began working as an investment manager for the Massachusetts Hospital Life Insurance Company. He advised his clients, many of whom had earned their fortunes as merchant sea captains, to invest in manufacturing and thereby helped prepare Massachusetts's transition from a maritime to an industrial economy, moving progress inland toward the textile centers of Lowell and Lawrence.

The major work of his later life was a monumental translation of French astronomer Pierre-Simon Laplace's five-volume work on the solar system, the *Méchanique Céleste*, originally published about the same time as the *Navigator*. Bowditch's translation was published in 1829.

Bowditch died in Boston in 1838. He is buried in Cambridge's Mount Auburn Cemetery underneath a life-sized bronze statue, the first to be cast in this country.

In 1955, author Jean Lee Latham published a fictionalized account of Bowditch's early life for young readers. *Carry On, Mr. Bowditch* won the Newbury Medal for an outstanding work of children's literature, which helped put the book on many elementary school children's reading lists. It is through this early introduction that Bowditch has become an archetype of early New England ingenuity and self-made success.

PLACES TO SEE

2 Kimball Court, Salem
This home, called the John Crowninshield house, once stood nearby at 14 Brown Street and is where Nathaniel Bowditch was born in 1773 to Habakkuk and Mary Ingersoll Bowditch. It is currently a private home and has been much expanded since the Bowditches' time.

12 Chestnut Street, Salem
Shortly after the publication of the *New American Practical Navigator*, the Bowditches moved into this home in the prosperous neighborhood now known as the McIntire Historic District. (Nathaniel Hawthorne and his family lived in the house next door at 18 Chestnut Street some forty years later.) It is not open to the public.

This three-story house on North Street was the Bowditch family's final home in Salem.

9 North Street, Salem
Bowditch lived in this home with his family from 1811 until 1823, when they moved to Boston for his job with the Massachusetts Hospital Life Insurance Company. The circa-1805, three-story clapboard house was located at 312 Essex Street when the Bowditches lived there, but it was moved to its present location when the street was widened in 1944. It is on the National Register of Historic Places and is currently in the process of being renovated as a center for research and education. It is adjacent to the Corwin Witch House, part of the same preservation effort that relocated the Bowditch House.

Walking Tour
The Salem National Maritime Historic Site publishes a walking tour that includes these and many other sites related to Bowditch, his family and his maritime life. It can be accessed online at www.nps.gov/sama/planyourvisit/brochures.htm.

NATHANIEL HAWTHORNE (1804–1864)

The aspect of the venerable mansion has always affected me like a human countenance, bearing the traces not merely of outward storm and sunshine, but expressive also, of the long lapse of mortal life, and accompanying vicissitudes that have passed within. Were these to be worthily recounted, they would form a narrative of no small interest and instruction, and possessing, moreover, a certain remarkable unity, which might almost seem the result of artistic arrangement.
—*Nathaniel Hawthorne,* The House of the Seven Gables

Salem's most renowned native son and one of the first men of American letters, Nathaniel Hawthorne was born on the Fourth of July 1804 and lived much of his life within blocks of Salem Common and the boulevard that now bears his name.

Born Nathaniel Hathorne, some argue that he added the *w* to his last name to distance himself from Hathorne ancestors who had presided over the Salem witch trials; others say it was simply to make the spelling agree with the pronunciation. His father died at sea when Hawthorne was just four years old, and he moved with his mother and two sisters to his maternal grandparents' house on Herbert Street. He had a tendency to be a recluse—after a childhood injury, he spent two years as an invalid even though doctors couldn't find anything physically wrong with him. An uncle insisted on sending him to Bowdoin College in Maine, despite Hawthorne's ambivalence. After graduating, he moved back in with his family and spent the next few years writing in his room, taking his meals there, going for nighttime walks and rarely socializing. He was extremely critical of his own work. His first novel, *Fanshawe*, was published anonymously in 1828, but he eventually disowned the work as not being up to snuff and asked his friends to destroy their copies of it.

Nathaniel Hawthorne, taken sometime between 1860 and 1865. *Courtesy Library of Congress, LC-DIG-cwpbh-03440.*

In 1842, Hawthorne married Sophia Peabody, the youngest sister of educators and intellectual scenesters Elizabeth and Mary Peabody, whose childhood home shared a backyard with that of Hawthorne's maternal grandparents. Sophia was also reclusive as a young woman, suffering from frequent migraines that her Unitarian mother ascribed to the sensitivity that was woman's lot after Adam's fall. Nathaniel and Sophia's temperaments were well suited—both were reserved, with a capacity for melancholy, but creative, well spoken and devoted to each other.

Hawthorne published many short stories in the following years but was not able to support his family (which, by 1846, included oldest daughter Una and son Julian) writing alone, and he accepted a job at the Salem Custom House. Working during the day at a bustling seaport was not conducive to his writing—especially after years in near seclusion while he honed his craft—and he struggled with the inability to produce anything of substance. He left the job, which was a political appointment, in 1848 and again tried to devote himself solely to writing. He achieved his first success with a novel when *The Scarlet Letter* was published in 1850. His harsh depiction of seventeenth-century Boston cemented an image of judgmental Puritanical morality in the public imagination and connected to his own fear that his Puritan ancestors would deeply disapprove of his frivolous career choice. *The House of the Seven Gables* followed in 1851, a gloomy novel about the Pyncheon family's suffering under the weight of their ancestry. The Turner-Ingersoll Mansion on Derby Street was the inspiration for the iconic Pyncheon home and now serves as the centerpiece of a National Historic Landmark campus that also includes Hawthorne's birthplace.

The family moved around to other Massachusetts towns over the next few years, eventually settling at Wayside in Concord, which served as home base even during Hawthorne's next political appointment. At the behest of his college friend President Franklin Pierce, he served as American consul in Liverpool and would spend the years 1853 to 1860 in Europe with his family. They returned to the Wayside, where Hawthorne published the only major work that he completed while in Europe, *The Marble Faun*, which was to be his last novel. Hawthorne died in his sleep in 1864 while traveling in New Hampshire with ex-president Pierce.

PLACES TO SEE

The House of the Seven Gables, 115 Derby Street, Salem
The 1668 Turner-Ingersoll Mansion that inspired *The House of the Seven Gables* was restored in 1910 and moved in 1958 to 115 Derby Street, where it now stands with other historic structures that tell the tales of Salem throughout three centuries of history: the Retire Becket House (1655, now the gift shop); the Hooper Hathaway House (1682, now offices); Nathaniel Hawthorne's Birthplace (circa 1750); the Phippen House (circa 1782, not open to the public); and the Counting House (circa 1830).

One of the oldest surviving seventeenth-century wooden mansions, the Turner-Ingersoll house was originally built in 1668 for Captain John Turner, who enhanced it with two additions

Turner-Ingersoll Mansion, the House of the Seven Gables. © *Elizabeth Thompsen*.

before his son, John Turner II, inherited the house in 1692. The third generation of John Turners lost the family's fortune and was forced to sell the house to the Ingersoll family—cousins of the Hawthornes. During the Ingersolls' tenure, some of John Turner's original additions were removed to keep the house more in line with Federal period tastes. When Hawthorne spent time there visiting his cousin Susanna Ingersoll, the house had only three gables. When embellishing the setting for his 1851 novel *The House of the Seven Gables*, Hawthorne mentally restored it to its seventeenth-century form.

Likewise, when philanthropist Caroline Emmerton purchased the house in 1908, planning to open it for tourists as a means to fund her charity work and an adjacent settlement house, she worked with preservation architect Joseph Everett Chandler to restore it to an idealized version of its original state. Recognizing that visitors would want to see a house reminiscent of the version they had read about in Hawthorne's story, she and Chandler renovated it in the

The window of Hepzibah Pyncheon's cent shop, as imagined at the House of the Seven Gables museum. © *gailf548*.

Colonial revival style and also added a cent shop like the one the fictional Hepzibah Pyncheon runs in the novel. She also added a secret staircase, which, although inauthentic, is one of the most interesting creepy-cool elements of the house and certainly fits in with the book's foreboding atmosphere. The house is furnished as the well-to-do Ingersolls would have dictated in the 1840s, the time period when Hawthorne would have known it firsthand. In addition to the secret staircase, don't miss the magnificent canopy bed in a second-floor bedroom that overlooks the harbor.

Nathaniel Hawthorne's birthplace before it was moved from Union Street, 1941. *Historic American Buildings Survey, photo by Frank O. Branzetti, courtesy Library of Congress, HABS MASS,5-SAL,44.*

Across the seaside colonial garden from the Turner-Ingersoll Mansion is Hawthorne's actual birthplace, built around 1750 at 27 Union Street. The church that owned the house announced plans to tear down the neglected structure in the 1950s, but Emmerton's organization purchased it for one dollar and moved it to the House of the Seven Gables campus. Its association with Hawthorne is its most significant quality. The Georgian structure itself is not one of Salem's best examples of that architectural style, but it has since been furnished with many objects that belonged to the author or are authentic antiques and offer a glimpse into his family history and domestic life during the early 1800s.

If you'd like to be able to linger and ask questions of the knowledgeable tour guides, avoid visiting during weekends in October, when thousands of tourists descend on Witch City for Halloween-themed sightseeing. On these weekends, admission lines at the House of the Seven Gables extend into the parking

Bela Pratt's bronze statue of Nathaniel Hawthorne on Hawthorne Boulevard in Salem.

lot, and the steady stream of tours means that groups are only allowed five minutes in each room.

Hawthorne Statue, Hawthorne Boulevard (near Essex Street), Salem

The Hawthorne Memorial Society commissioned this full-size bronze statue from sculptor Bela Pratt in the 1910s. It was dedicated in 1925, about the same time that the nearby Hawthorne Hotel was completed.

10½–12 Herbert Street, Salem

This was Hawthorne's most frequent residence between 1808 and 1840, except for periods away at college in Maine and at other Salem homes with his mother and sisters. After falling on difficult financial circumstances in 1845, he was forced to live here again briefly, this time with his wife. Most of his early stories were written in his third-floor room of what he called Castle Dismal. He wrote, "I sat a long, long time waiting patiently for the world to know me."[44]

54 Charter Street, Salem

Hawthorne's wife, Sophia, lived here with her parents, three brothers and two sisters—Elizabeth Palmer Peabody and Mary Peabody Mann—when she and Hawthorne courted. His unfinished novels *The Dolliver Romance* and *Dr. Grimshawe's Secret* are set in this house. The building is not open to the public, but the original door is now located at the back entrance of the Phillips Library at the Peabody Essex Museum, 134 Essex Street, Salem.

Salem's Custom House, where Hawthorne worked in the 1840s. © *Paul Keleher*.

Custom House, 169 Derby Street, Salem
Hawthorne was already a published author when he took a position as surveyor at the Salem Custom House. The Custom House is open to the public as part of the Salem Maritime National Historic Site, where you can see artifacts such as the stencil he used to mark incoming cargo that he had assessed.

18 Chestnut Street, Salem
Known as the Botts-Faben House, Hawthorne lived here, on what his wife called "the most stately street in Salem," from

Hawthorne and his family lived at 18 Chestnut Street while he worked at the Custom House.

1846 to 1847. This may be the oldest house on Chestnut Street, although documentation is incomplete.[45] The private home is closed to the public.

Essex Mall Fountain, Salem
At the center of a contemporary fountain on the Essex Mall pedestrian way is the old town pump made famous in Hawthorne's short story, "A Rill from the Town Pump," part of the volume *Twice-Told Tales.*

14 Mall Street, Salem
This was Hawthorne's final Salem residence before moving to Concord and then Europe. Here, his third-floor room was not Castle

Hawthorne's final Salem residence on Mall Street.

Dismal, but a quiet retreat, "as if among the stars," according to Sophia. It was here that he wrote *The Scarlet Letter,* and a plaque on what is now a multifamily private home stands as testament to this spot on the American literary map.

Salem Athenaeum, 337 Essex Street, Salem
The athenaeum contains works by Salem authors, including first editions and the early lending libraries used by Nathaniel Hawthorne.

Salem Lyceum, 43 Church Street, Salem
This former lecture hall hosted talks by the likes of Henry David Thoreau and Ralph Waldo Emerson. For more than sixty years, speakers held forth on subjects including history, literature, science, religion and politics "for mutual education and rational entertainment." Hawthorne himself never lectured here (rumor is that he was too shy about public speaking), but he did serve as the lecture series secretary in 1848. Today, the historic building is home to the stylish Lyceum Bar & Grill.

Walking Tour

The Salem National Maritime Historic Site publishes an in-depth, self-guided walking tour that includes these and many other sites related to Hawthorne, his life in Salem and his books. It can be accessed online at www.nps.gov/sama/planyourvisit/brochures. htm. In 2008, Jonathan Hardy Wright published *Hawthorne's Haunts in New England*, a pictorial tour of the many places where Hawthorne lived and worked in the North Shore and beyond, and excellent further reading if this walking tour whets your appetite.

ELIZABETH PALMER PEABODY (1804–1894) AND MARY PEABODY MANN (1807–1887)

To be a [kindergarten teacher] *is the perfect development of womanliness—a working with God at the very fountain of artistic and intellectual power and moral character.*
—*Elizabeth Palmer Peabody*[46]

Elizabeth and Mary Peabody, along with their younger sister Sophia, were among Salem's most influential and intellectual women in the nineteenth century.

The oldest of Eliza and Nathaniel Peabody's three daughters, Elizabeth Palmer Peabody moved with her family to Salem when she was four years old. From the Peabodys' modest lodgings on Union Street near Salem's waterfront, Elizabeth was immediately drawn into a world of education and culture as she watched and then assisted her mother with teaching school. Her father taught her Latin, the first of ten languages that Elizabeth would learn over her lifetime. All of the Peabody children were raised with their mother's strong Unitarian beliefs, which they maintained throughout their lives.

As Elizabeth grew older, she met authors like Nathaniel Hawthorne, who would later marry her youngest sister, Sophia. By the time she was thirty, Elizabeth had opened and run two of her own schools and worked at Bronson Alcott's Temple School in Boston, where she became involved with the transcendentalist movement. Later, she opened the nation's first English-language kindergarten (the concept had been brought to America by German-speaking immigrants) in Boston's Beacon Hill neighborhood.

Elizabeth Peabody's literary contributions include *Reminiscences of Rev. William Ellery Channing*, *Record of a School* (Bronson Alcott's school) and *A Last Evening with Allston* (the painter Washington Allston). She was among America's first female publishers—for two years she edited and published *The Dial*, the journal of the Transcendentalists. She also published antislavery material and children's books by Nathaniel Hawthorne, as well as the first appearance of Thoreau's "Essay on Civil Disobedience" in her short-lived journal *Aesthetic Papers*. Her bookstore on West Street in Boston became famous for the prominent literary and political figures who held "Conversations" for women about important issues there. The reformer Margaret Fuller was just one of the luminaries who participated.

Mary Peabody, the second of the three Peabody sisters, shared Elizabeth's passion for education and writing. In 1843, she married Horace Mann, widely considered the father of public education in America. After her husband's early death in 1859, Mary Mann joined Elizabeth's efforts to establish the kindergarten movement. Together they wrote *Moral Culture of Infancy and Kindergarten Guide*, and were largely responsible for editing and publishing *The Kindergarten Messenger*, the movement's newspaper, from 1873 to 1875. Mary Mann also published a biography of her late husband, a romance set in Cuba based on her stay there in the 1830s with her sister Sophia and books on the plight of the Piute Indian tribe.

Megan Marshall's 2005 biography, *The Peabody Sisters: Three Women Who Ignited American Romanticism*, tells the story of these influential siblings. *Publisher's Weekly* writes:

> *Marshall has distilled 20 years of research into a book that brings the sisters to life, along with their extended family and*

friends, and the time in which they matured: a time, Marshall notes, that allowed women to be on a more equal footing than they would enjoy later in the century.

It is an in-depth look at the women who were at the center of a uniquely creative time in the arts and letters of the young nation.

PLACES TO SEE

Home of Elizabeth Peabody and Mary Peabody Mann (corner of Union and Essex Streets), Salem
This building, known by the names Brown Building, Merchant's Building or Union Building, is where the Peabody family moved in 1808, when the daughters were young children, just before Sophia was born.

54 Charter Street, Salem
The Peabody family's home at 54 Charter Street is not open to the public, but its original doorway is located at the back entrance of the Phillips Library at the Peabody Essex Museum, 134 Essex Street, Salem.

JONES VERY (1813–1880)

His talents are of a high order…Is he insane? If so, there yet linger glimpses of wisdom in his memory. He is insane with God—diswitted in the contemplation of the holiness of Divinity.
—Bronson Alcott, 1838[47]

Jones Very was a little-known essayist and poet of intensely pious Shakespearean sonnets whose mysticism fascinated the Transcendentalists in the 1830s and '40s.

Very was born in Salem in 1813 to Captain Jones Very and his first cousin Lydia Very, who never married. Aside from a two-year sea voyage during which the nine-year-old Jones visited Kronborg Castle—the setting for *Hamlet* and the catalyst for a lifelong fascination with the character—he had little contact with his father, who died when Jones was eleven.

Raising Jones and his five siblings essentially as a single mother, Lydia Very was passionately, smotheringly protective of her children. Despite her vehement and alienating atheism, Very immersed himself in Unitarian study while attending Harvard and developed a zealous spirituality that found some kinship in the principles of transcendentalism then emerging from contemporaries like Ralph Waldo Emerson.

He caught the attention of Elizabeth Palmer Peabody and the "incestuous community of New England intelligentsia,"[48] and she brought him into a literary circle that included Emerson, Bronson Alcott and Nathaniel Hawthorne. Though these men were intrigued by Very, his spiritual devotion was becoming more eccentric and more ascetic. Tormented by desire, he vowed not only to avoid the company of women, but also to avoid even looking at them. He was completing his landmark essay on Shakespeare at this time (whom he regarded as divinely inspired), as well as tutoring at Harvard Divinity School. But he was beginning to show signs of either extreme divine inspiration of his own or of a mental breakdown.

He came to fervently believe that he had submerged his will so fully that God controlled his every action. His increasingly emphatic belief that he was the second coming of Christ led to his dismissal from Harvard Divinity School. He returned home to live with his mother, whom he was finally able to convert to Christianity. His other attempts at persuasive conversion were less successful. After a time of trying to baptize his literary colleagues, as well as the local clergy, the Reverend Charles Wentworth Upham (who was already opposed to the transcendental tenets that Very was seeking to embody with his devout Christianity) finally had him forcibly committed to an asylum. He was deemed harmless and soon released.

Emerson, though wary of his friend's evangelism, still offered to edit Very's volume of essays and poems. But when he offered editorial suggestions, Very became extremely agitated, believing that since he was merely transcribing God's word, the work was beyond reproach. To this, Emerson replied, "Cannot the spirit parse & spell?"[49] Not long after the volume's publication—it went largely unnoticed—Very's divinity came to an end. As suddenly as it had come upon him, the winds of religious zeal died down, and the man who once insisted that he was Jesus reincarnate eventually lived out his life in relative quiet and anonymity.

PLACES TO SEE

Old South Cemetery, Main Street, Peabody
Very is buried in the family plot at Old South Cemetery in Peabody. His sister Lydia, a noted children's book illustrator, is interred there, too.

KATE TANNATT WOODS (1836–1910)

Author, editor and journalist Woods founded the Thought and Work Club in 1891 with the goal of encouraging "women in all departments of literary work, to promote home study, and to secure literary and social advantages for its members." In Salem, she was involved in founding numerous women's clubs and wrote prolifically for publications including *Harper's Bazaar*, *Ladies Home Journal* and the *Boston Transcript* on subjects from the need for more comprehensive American history education to early Moravian customs.

PLACES TO SEE

36 Lynde Street, Salem
The tearoom in which the Thought and Work Club met for many years was on this spot near the corner of Essex Street just north of the McIntire Historic District. The building is no longer in existence.

166 North Street, Salem
Woods called her home on North Street Maple Rest.

CHARLOTTE FORTEN GRIMKÉ (1837–1914)

The long, dark night of the past, with all its sorrows and its fears, was forgotten; and for the Future—the eyes of these freed children see no clouds in it. It is full of sunlight, they think, and they trust in it, perfectly.
—*Charlotte Forten Grimké in "Life on the Sea Islands"*

One of the earliest students to attend Salem Normal School—designed to educate young women for teaching careers—was Charlotte Forten, an African American woman from Philadelphia. Her grandfather was an ardent abolitionist, and the family was well acquainted with activists like William Lloyd Garrison and John Greenleaf Whittier. Charlotte was home-schooled rather than be allowed to attend Philadelphia's segregated schools, but when she was sixteen, Forten was sent north to Salem because the schools there were desegregated. She lived with the Remond family, prominent members of Salem's African American community. Forten was the only nonwhite member of her class at the Higginson Grammar School, and in 1856 she became the first African American to graduate the Salem Normal School. After graduation she worked for the integrated Epes Grammar School, where she became the first African American to teach white students.

Forten also wrote poetry and kept a journal for most of her life, documenting her experiences as a free black woman in the antebellum North. Despite frustrations about slavery that drove her to question Christianity, she rechanneled her anger into teaching. She became involved in the Sea Islands Mission, where she taught the children of freed slaves on St. Helena Island off the coast of South Carolina. She struggled with her feeling of disconnection from these children, most of whom were only recently freed slaves and spoke only the Gullah language. As a young woman from a wealthy northern family who had always lived as a free citizen, she had more in common with her white colleagues. Her account of this experience was published in the *Atlantic Monthly* in 1864, but her most lasting literary contribution is her journal, in which she wrote almost daily until after her return from South Carolina and resumed toward the end of her life.

She retired from teaching after her time at the Sea Islands Mission and returned to Philadelphia, where she met and married the Presbyterian minister Francis Grimké, thirteen years her junior. The couple's only child died in infancy, but they remained married until Charlotte's death in 1914 at age seventy-six. Together they continued to champion causes of racial equality, embodying one of Francis's most repeated statements, "Race prejudice can't be talked down, it must be lived down."

PLACES TO SEE

Salem Normal School (corner of Broad and Summer Streets), Salem
The Salem Normal School eventually evolved into today's Salem State College on Lafayette Street. Its original location is now a city-owned office building.

Lydia Pinkham

Although Lydia Pinkham's famous Vegetable Compound may have had only dubious medicinal properties, the famous marketer's name also adorns a women's clinic in Salem, established in her honor by her only daughter.

Places to See

Lydia Pinkham Memorial Clinic, 250 Derby Street, Salem
Built by Pinkham's daughter Aroline Chase Gove in 1922, the clinic is still in operation in this Colonial revival building.

ANDOVER

Incorporated in 1646, Andover's early history is marked by Native American attacks during King Philip's War, as well as involvement in the Salem witch trials, during which more than forty Andover residents were accused. Today, its most well-known feature is Phillips Academy, the prestigious boarding school founded in 1778.

If you're a book buff who is also interested in the history of printing and typography, check out the Museum of Printing at 800 Massachusetts Avenue. The museum was founded to save printing equipment throughout history, from letterpress printing to photographic and electronic technologies. The museum tells the stories of these changes using one of the world's largest collections of printing hardware.

ANNE BRADSTREET

Although she is most closely associated with Ipswich, Anne Bradstreet and her family ultimately settled on a farm in North

Andover, which is where Bradstreet died in 1672 at the age of sixty-one.

PLACES TO SEE

Old Burying Ground, Academy Road, Andover
The location of Bradstreet's grave is not certain, but a monument stands in a far corner of the Old Burying Ground. From Osgood Street, turn left onto Academy Road. The cemetery is just ahead on the right, with the entrance at a break in the low stone wall just past the intersection of Academy and Court Streets. A plaque on the stone wall marks the cemetery's dedication in 1660. The monument, placed by the Andover Historical Society in 2002, is to the left, near the farthest corner of this well-maintained burial ground.

Used until the 1800s, the grounds near Stevens Pond contain many centuries-old headstones and are a reflective place for history buffs to stroll. This spot also marks the center of Andover's original settlement. Local records at the Stevens Memorial Library, about half a mile away at 345 Main Street, can help you identify other notable figures also buried here. (Anne's husband, Simon Bradstreet, is buried in Salem's Old Burying Point, although the Anne who lies next to him there is likely his second wife, who shared the poet's given name.)

HARRIET BEECHER STOWE (1811–1896)

The story was not the work of a novice, and it was written out of abundant experience and from an immense mass of accumulated thought and material. She was in the maturity of her intellectual powers, she was trained in the art of writing, and she had…abundant store of materials on which to draw. To be sure, she was on fire with a moral

purpose, but she had the dramatic instinct, and she felt that her object would not be reached by writing an abolition tract.
—*Charles Dudley Warner*[50]

As one of America's first bestselling authors, Harriet Beecher Stowe's literary output was plentiful, but her first novel, the groundbreaking *Uncle Tom's Cabin*, remains her best-known and most influential work.

Harriet was the seventh of thirteen children born to Presbyterian preacher and seminary scholar Lyman Beecher, and she spent her early life in Connecticut, where she eventually taught and wrote with her sister Catharine, founder of the Hartford Seminary for Women. Although a number of Harriet's siblings, most notably the theologian Henry Ward Beecher, became prominent in the abolitionist movement, their domineering father was not known for liberal views. The family moved to what was then still the dusty outpost town of Cincinnati when Lyman was named president of Lane Theological Seminary. He famously opposed his students' wishes and refused to admit African Americans to Lane. About fifty students left the seminary in protest, adding fuel to the growing and divisive fire of abolitionist action leading up to the Civil War.

Harriet Beecher Stowe, circa 1880. *Courtesy Library of Congress, LC-USZ62-11212.*

While living in Ohio, Harriet earned a modest living by writing short stories, essays and poetry for magazines, work she continued even after marrying Lane teacher Calvin Ellis Stowe and giving birth to four children within four years.

The passage of the Fugitive Slave Law in 1850—declaring that any runaway slave must be returned to his or her master, regardless of what state of the union the slave had been found in—was a major catalyst for the abolitionist movement. Many northerners who had previously disagreed with slavery but felt it was an issue that didn't affect them directly now felt that their own rights were being eroded by the "slaveocracy" of the southern states. Some simply opposed the infringement on state's rights, but many began to see more and more clearly the cruelty of slavery. The Stowes were by now living in Brunswick, Maine, where Calvin was teaching at Bowdoin College. A letter from Stowe's sister-in-law, in which she wrote, "Harriet, if I could use a pen as you can, I would write something that would make this whole nation feel what an accursed thing slavery is," was the encouragement Stowe needed to begin *Uncle Tom's Cabin*.

The book began as fictional sketches, drawing on extensive interviews with fugitive slaves, former and current slaveholders, those who helped fleeing slaves reach the North and many others who were directly affected by and involved in the slave trade. William Lloyd Garrison, the editor of the zealously abolitionist Newburyport paper the *Liberator*, helped Stowe place these sketches in the Cincinnati paper the *National Era*. The stories were so affecting and popular that in 1852 she collected them in a two-volume book, which sold an unheard-of 350,000 copies in its first year.

In *Uncle Tom's Cabin*, she drew on her own experience of losing a child to cholera to imagine the grief that a slave mother must feel in being forcibly separated from her children:

> *If it were your Harry, mother, or your Willie, that were going to be torn from you by a brutal trader, tomorrow morning,—if you had seen the man, and heard that the papers were signed and delivered, and you had only from twelve o'clock till morning to make good your escape,—how fast could you walk? How many*

miles could you make in those few brief hours, with the darling at your bosom,—the little sleepy head on your shoulder,—the small, soft arms trustingly holding on to your neck?

In this way she made the realities of a life of slavery tangible to a large audience, many of whom felt able to empathize with African American characters for the first time.

PLACES TO SEE

Stowe House, 80 Bartlet Street, Andover

In 1862, as Stowe was preparing *Uncle Tom's Cabin* for publication, Calvin Stowe accepted a job teaching at Andover Theological Seminary, and the family moved into this large stone house (then on Chapel Avenue) that was formerly the seminary's carpenter shop. It was while living here that Stowe finished work on *Uncle Tom's Cabin* and shortly thereafter wrote *A Key to Uncle Tom's Cabin*, intended to rebut southern parodies championing slavery and claiming that she had not researched her topic.

Stowe House on the Phillips Andover campus.

In 1908, Andover Theological Seminary moved to Cambridge, and its properties were purchased by Phillips Academy. The Stowe House was moved in 1928 to its present location, where it remains as student housing. It is not open to the public but is easily viewed from the sidewalk and is a quick detour to make en route to the Stowes' graves in the cemetery at Phillips Academy.

Phillips Academy Cemetery, Chapel Avenue, Andover
The family lived in Andover until Calvin's retirement in 1864, when they moved for the last time to Hartford, Connecticut. It was in Hartford that both Calvin and Harriet passed away, he in 1894 and she in 1896. Both are buried near some of their children on the grounds of Phillips Academy.

The cemetery is past the Andover Inn and Addison Gallery on Chapel Avenue, behind Samuel Phillips Hall. Harriet Stowe's grave is near the center of the small cemetery, marked by a tall red granite obelisk.

Harriet Beecher Stowe's grave on the Phillips Andover campus.

ELIZABETH STUART PHELPS (1815–1852) AND ELIZABETH STUART PHELPS WARD (1844–1911)

*Write, if you must; not otherwise. Do not write, if you can earn a
fair living at teaching or dressmaking, at electricity or hod-carrying.
Make shoes, weed cabbages, survey land, keep house, make ice-cream,
sell cake, climb a telephone pole. Nay, be a lightning-rod peddler or a
book agent, before you set your heart upon it that you shall write for a
living…Living? It is more likely to be dying by your pen; despairing
by your pen; burying hope and heart and youth and courage in your
ink-stand.*
—*Elizabeth Stuart Phelps Ward*[51]

Both Elizabeth Stuart Phelps and her daughter Elizabeth
Stuart Phelps Ward were prolific, reform-minded authors who
published religious and moral series for children in addition to
adult fiction.

Born in 1815, the elder Elizabeth grew up in Andover, where
she wrote stories to entertain her siblings. As a student at Boston's
Mount Vernon School, she studied with Jacob Abbott, the author
of the Rollo and Lucy series of children's fiction—the first such
series ever published in the United States. Taking the pseudonym
H. Trusta (an anagram of Stuart), Elizabeth published a few
stories in various magazines before marrying the clergyman Austin
Phelps, giving birth to daughter Mary Gray and returning to live
in Andover.

After the birth of a son in 1848, Elizabeth began writing the
Kitty Brown series of religious juvenile fiction. She published four
Kitty books in four years, while also turning out volumes of stories
for her own children, many of which were published posthumously
by her husband. Among her adult fiction, the semiautobiographical
A Peep at Number Five was popular in its day. Sadly, she passed away

in 1852 shortly after the birth of a second son, who was baptized at her funeral.

In her mother's honor, Mary Gray Phelps took her name and became the second Elizabeth Stuart Phelps. The younger woman shared her mother's gift of imagination even as a child and began publishing stories by the age of thirteen. Her Gypsy Breynton series for young women introduced one of the first tomboyish little girls to American children's fiction, an archetype followed by Jo March and Laura Ingalls through to today's Ramona Quimby and Junie B. Jones.

Gypsy climbed out of the window without the slightest hesitation, and walked along the ridge-pole with the ease and fearlessness of a boy. She had on a pretty blue delaine dress, which was wet and torn, and all stuck together with burs; her boots were covered with mud to the ankle; her white stockings spattered and brown; her turban was hanging round her neck by its elastic; her net had come off, and the wind was blowing her hair all over her eyes; she had her sack thrown over one arm, and a basket filled to overflowing, with flowers and green moss, upon the other.

In 1868, the *Atlantic Monthly* published her story "The Tenth of January," about a fire at the Pemberton Textile Mill in Lawrence in 1860 that killed seven hundred workers. John Greenleaf Whittier read the story and offered Phelps her first piece of encouragement from a literary peer.[52] It was with her 1868 novel *Gates Ajar* that the younger Phelps achieved her greatest fame as an author. Of the novel's contemporaries, only Harriet Beecher Stowe's *Uncle Tom's Cabin*, published fifteen years earlier, sold more copies. Over the next two decades she published a number of feminist articles and was the first woman to lecture at Boston University.

In 1888, at age forty-four, she scandalously married the journalist Herbert Dickinson Ward, the much younger son of a family friend. The two published several romances together, and Phelps Ward continued to champion reform causes, including a later-life crusade against vivisection. She died in 1911 and is buried in Newtown, Massachusetts.

PLACES TO SEE

Phelps Home, 189 Main Street, Andover

Elizabeth Stuart Phelps Ward's home is now part of the Phillips Academy campus. As of 2008, the school is not actively using the building, although the grounds are immaculately maintained. A quick stroll through the rear garden path to peek at the small summerhouse, massive back porch and outdoor fireplace would be unlikely to disturb any staff or students. It is difficult to see the house number from the street; the building has yellow siding and a green front door.

Elizabeth Stuart Phelps Ward's house on the Phillips Andover campus.

HAVERHILL

Although Haverhill began as a farming community, it quickly benefitted from the power source of the Merrimack River as a center for sawmills, gristmills, tanneries and shipbuilding. Like nearby Lynn, it was home to a large shoemaking industry for almost two hundred years. Today, technology and research flourish in the city's industrial parks.

One of Haverhill's most notable residents was the poet and activist John Greenleaf Whittier, whose family homestead is now open to the public. Just fifty years before the poet was born in 1807, the border between New Hampshire and Massachusetts was redrawn, as was the border between the towns of Methuen to the west and Haverhill to the east. Haverhill lost one-third of its population to New Hampshire and one-half of its land to Methuen, a serious reorganizing of the town's assets and people that must have affected the Whittier family and their neighbors well into the next generation.

John Greenleaf Whittier

Garrison at once rode to this secluded locality, which has since become so well known to the readers of Snow Bound, where he found the youthful poet, a bashful boy, at work with his father, who, though a man of excellent sense...was decidedly utilitarian in his views, and was anything but pleased with the literary tastes of his son. Mr. Garrison earnestly entreated him to place no restraints upon the poetical tendencies of the gifted boy who stood before him, little dreaming that he was destined to be an efficient co-laborer in the reform to which he was about consecrating the best years of his life, and that the poet would live to celebrate in immortal verse the downfall of American Slavery.
—Boston Commonwealth, *January 3, 1872*

As a child growing up on his family's farm on the outskirts of Haverhill, John Greenleaf Whittier showed more aptitude for reading than farming and was encouraged by a local schoolmaster, who introduced Whittier to the work of Scottish farmer-poet Robert Burns.

When he was a teenager, his sister Mary began anonymously sending his poems to the Newburyport *Free Press*, then edited by William Lloyd Garrison. Garrison published them, and Mary sent more. Eventually Garrison—who was only two years older than Whittier—tracked down the unnamed author and convinced him that his work was so promising that he should continue his schooling. This meeting would be providential, as Garrison eventually gave Whittier his first newspaper job and later encouraged him to throw his full support behind the antislavery movement, a cause that Whittier was already sympathetic to because of his Quaker upbringing.

In 1836, Whittier's brother married a non-Quaker woman and therefore felt unable to bring her to the family's homestead. Unable to maintain the farm without his brother's help, the two sold the property, and Whittier bought a house on Friend Street in Amesbury, where he moved with his sister, mother and an elderly aunt.

Although he rarely wrote about Haverhill in his youth, his later poems often looked back on his childhood on the farm. The best known of these—both in its time and now—is the long poem *Snow-Bound* published in 1866.

PLACES TO SEE

Whittier Homestead, 305 Whittier Road, Haverhill
At the John Greenleaf Whittier Homestead in Haverhill, the curator and caretaker welcomes visitors into the front room of the poet's childhood home. Sitting around the very fireplace that warmed the family during the 1817 blizzard recalled in *Snow-Bound*, visitors are treated to a practiced and knowledgeable story telling about Whittier's life and career.

The Whittier Society acquired the home in 1891, along with a great many pieces of furniture and décor that are not only authentic

John Greenleaf Whittier Homestead in Haverhill.

John Greenleaf Whittier Homestead in Haverhill, interior.

period pieces, but also were actually in the house when the poet lived there from 1807 to 1836. A bookshelf in the front room bows under the weight of 115 years of guest registers that record the name of everyone who has visited the homestead since it opened as a public museum in 1893.

The John Greenleaf Whittier Homestead is open year-round and is just as welcoming in the wintertime as it is in milder weather. Its vast, snow-covered lawn and icy Fernside brook running along the south of the property offer the kind of picturesque view of rural New England that Robert Frost made so iconic in his "Stopping by Woods on a Snowy Evening" more than fifty years after Whittier's own *Snow-Bound*.

Inside the house, don't miss the vibrant crazy quilt in the step-up bedroom, embroidered with hummingbirds and flowers, along with the names and initials of all the family members who worked in it. The parlor holds a collection of the books that first inspired the poet, including a volume of Robert Burns poems that he carried with him until the day he died. The homestead's curator knows the details of the home inside and out—she lives on the property as caretaker; this is no sterile museum—so don't be afraid to ask about anything that catches your eye.

Haverhill Public Library, 99 Main Street, Haverhill
The Whittier Collection in the library's Trustee Room has an extensive collection of books, manuscripts, paintings and more relating to Whittier's Quaker faith and abolitionism. The collection is available by appointment only.

WINFIELD TOWNLEY SCOTT (1910–1968)

Ignoring the Bomb, the Beats, the Beatles, and other forces of change and disintegration, a small group of American poets continues to write mild, mellow verse in the Concord manner of Emerson and Thoreau.

> *Their themes are hill and dale, solitude and sadness; their tone is*
> *elegiac; and the best of them is Winfield Townley Scott.*
> —Time *review of* Change of Weather, *1964*[53]

Haverhill poet Winfield Townley Scott showed promise even as a high school student and fell into literary circles as an undergraduate at Brown University in Providence, Rhode Island. For more than twenty years, he was the well-respected book page editor for the *Providence Journal*, while writing poems and keeping detailed and imaginative notebooks. His work deals with the people and places of his native New England, and much of the conflict comes from his own difficulty in reconciling a middle-class upbringing with the man-of-letters lifestyle that his work and his marriage to a woman of independent wealth enabled him to lead.

The title poem in his 1948 volume *Mr. Whittier* addresses the famous local poet whose reputation casts a long shadow over their shared hometown and takes some pleasure at imagining his great predecessor's foibles. In contrast to the women who remember, as children, "pears and apples / Given them by the famous, tamed, white-bearded saint," Scott writes:

> *Of course there is the old man—and I for one am grateful—who*
> *Recalls the seedy coat, the occasionally not so clean high collar,*
> *And that like many another he read his paper by the hour in*
> *   the privy,*
> *Carl Schurz, finding him rained in by the stove at the village store,*
> *Thought "So superior to those about him, yet so like them"*

Of course, at the end, Whittier earns Scott's respect for the ways in which the elder poet's verse gave modest Haverhill a place in the American literary tradition:

> *He put the names of our places into his poems and he honored*
> *   us with himself;*
> *And it is for us but not altogether, because larger than us.*

In his 1974 poem "The Reduction of Winfield Townley Scott," Dave Smith calls him a poet "of sensational skill but little sales," an observation that was unfortunately true. Although he was well liked, both his personal life and his work betrayed a mid-century sense of self-doubt. His *Collected Poems: 1937–1962* was well received—critics felt that he was in line with modern American poets, including William Carlos Williams[54]—but it was commercially unsuccessful. When the volume was remaindered at bookshops, Scott took it as a failure. His death at age fifty-eight, from a combination of alcohol and sleeping pills after a quarrel with his wife, was ruled a suicide.

PLACES TO SEE

Haverhill Public Library, 99 Main Street, Haverhill
For his contributions to literature, including his posthumously published journals, Scott is one of the townspeople honored in the library's Haverhill Citizen's Hall of Fame on the first floor.

BOB MONTANA (1920–1975)

Bob Montana was the creator of the extremely popular Archie comic series, which was largely based on classmates, faculty and situations he experienced as a student at Haverhill High School in the late 1930s. Montana spent his early childhood traveling the vaudeville circuit with his family, warming up the crowd with lasso tricks before his father's banjo act. By his teen years, his father had settled the family in Haverhill, where he ran a theatrical supply shop. It was there that Montana began sketching the people and places that would eventually populate Archie's hometown of Riverdale.

According to *Boston Globe* reporter Mark Sullivan, Crown Confectionery and the Chocolate Shop on Merrimack Street and the Tuscarora on Winter Street inspired Archie's Chok'lit Shop.[55] Although the soda fountains are all long gone, Haverhill High School still stands, looking much like its comic book counterpart. The Archie comics were also a family affair. Sullivan quotes Montana's daughter Lynn, "All of us kids would write down something that happened in school and put it in a box in the kitchen. If Dad used it, we got 25 cents. In those days that was a lot of money."[56]

PLACES TO SEE

Haverhill High School, 137 Monument Street, Haverhill
HHS was the original Riverdale High, although principal Earl MacLeod (fictionalized as Mr. Weatherbee) and librarian Elizabeth Tuck (aka Miss Grundy) have long since passed away.

Haverhill Public Library, 99 Main Street, Haverhill
A copy of Bob Montana's high school diary, in which he first sketched his friends and teachers, is kept in the library's archives. Montana is also honored in the Haverhill Citizen's Hall of Fame, located on the library's first floor, alongside such fellow townspeople as John Greenleaf Whittier, founder of Metro Goldwyn-Mayer Louis B. Mayer and colonial heroine Hannah Emerson Dustin.

ANDRE DUBUS II (1936–1999)

Although he was born and raised in Louisiana, short story author Andre Dubus lived his adult life in Haverhill and set much of his acclaimed fiction in the Merrimack Valley. His work often chronicles the struggles of contemporary men whose lives have gone wrong for reasons they can't comprehend, and his characters often share the author's own strong Catholic faith. His collections include

Andre Dubus II. *Courtesy Random House.*

Adultery and Other Choices (1977), *The Times Are Never So Bad* (1983) and *Dancing After Hours* (1996).

In 1986, Dubus was helping a brother and sister who had been in a car accident on the highway when another car swerved and hit all three of them. The young man died, the woman lived only because Dubus pushed her out of the way and the author suffered injuries that left him in a wheelchair for the rest of his life. His essay collection *Meditations from a Movable Chair* (1998) is a frank reflection of the pain and difficulty of his injuries. In part to repay the generosity of his community after the accident, he held free weekly writing workshops in his home until his death in 1999.

LAWRENCE

Once one of northeastern Massachusetts's most prosperous industrial towns, Lawrence was home to massive textile mills powered by the Merrimack River. The city's most famous man of letters, Robert Frost, spent his adolescence here because his grandfather was a mill overseer.

Lawrence has been called "Immigrant City" since the early nineteenth century. Irish, German, French Canadian, Italian and Eastern European immigrants came in the mid-nineteenth century to work in the mills. Lebanese, Jewish and Polish families added to the mix around the turn of the twentieth century. Today, Lawrence ranks among the nation's largest Latino populations (68 percent in 2006),[57] and the brightly painted storefronts of Dominican bodegas and Puerto Rican hair salons provide a welcome, colorful contrast to New England winters. The city's Dominican Independence Day festival in August is a large community affair that frequently honors Lawrence's most prominent Dominican American citizens. The 2008 festival celebrated the late Jose Balbuena, who ran the Nobel Book Store on Haverhill Street for many years.

ROBERT FROST (1874–1963)

"I have been," he wrote, "one acquainted with the night." And because he knew the midnight as well as the high noon, because he understood the ordeal as well as the triumph of the human spirit, he gave his age strength with which to overcome despair. At bottom, he held a deep faith in the spirit of man, and it is hardly an accident that Robert Frost coupled poetry and power, for he saw poetry as the means of saving power from itself.
—*President John F. Kennedy at the dedication of the Robert Frost Library, Amherst College, October 1963*

Robert Frost's evocative and unaffected verse has done much to define an image of pastoral New England life for readers across the globe. While he is most closely associated with his homestead in Franconia, New Hampshire (now a museum and poetry conference center known as the Frost Place), and with the Bread Loaf Writers' Conference at Middlebury College in Vermont, his earliest years in

Robert Frost, 1941. *Courtesy Library of Congress, LC-USZ62-120743.*

New England were spent in the industrial town of Lawrence along the Merrimack River.

Frost was born in San Francisco in 1874, but after his father's death in 1885 he moved with his mother to her hometown of Lawrence, where his grandfather was a supervisor at the Lower Pacific Mill on Appleton Street. After high school, where he first felt his calling as a poet, he attended Dartmouth College but didn't graduate. Returning to Lawrence, he worked odd jobs while submitting poems to newspapers. In 1894, just two years after he graduated from high school, he sold "My Butterfly: An Elegy" to the New York *Independent* and, buoyed by his first taste of success, proposed to his high school sweetheart Elinor White. After Elinor finished college and Frost attended Harvard (again, not long enough to graduate), the two were married and moved to a farm in Derry, New Hampshire, ending Frost's days as a New England city boy.

PLACES TO SEE

Walking Trail
The Robert Frost Foundation maintains a walking trail of historic sites in the poet's life, but only the most devoted fans of his work would make a special trip for this itinerary. Many of these minor landmarks are no longer standing. The Central Building on Essex Street, where his mother lived and ran a school and where Frost married his wife Elinor, is now a run-down office building, and the YMCA now stands where Elinor's childhood home once was. It would be far more worthwhile to time a visit with one of the many talks and programs that the foundation runs throughout the summer months.

However, the centerpiece of the walking tour and of downtown's Campagnone Common is the bubbling Robert Frost Fountain, a sculptural recreation of a woodland brook shaded by birch trees. Downtown Lawrence is quiet on the weekends, and in the summer the common is a pleasant place to stroll or let kids loose on the playground. Visit the Frost Foundation online at www.frostfoundation.org.

LOWELL

Farther to the west in the Merrimack Valley, the industrial boomtown of Lowell is well worth a visit for any literature buff. This was Jack Kerouac's hometown, a place he wrote about and referenced often in novels and poetry throughout his life.

Founded in 1826, Lowell was designed to be an industrial center for the then-burgeoning textile mills. The city thrived into the early twentieth century, as attested to by many of the impressive civic buildings and architecture downtown. But, in a story familiar to every town that counted on the power of the Merrimack River to turn its economy, the decline in manufacturing jobs in the twentieth century led to a severe economic downturn in Lowell. More than many of its neighbors, though, Lowell has rebounded in recent years by embracing its mill history through museums and public programs; by repurposing mill buildings into spacious loft housing and offices; and by encouraging an arts scene that has begun to thrive as an alternative to more expensive outlets in nearby Boston and Cambridge.

LUCY LARCOM (1824–1894)

The ninth of ten children of a shipmaster father, Lucy Larcom was born in 1824 in Beverly. As a child she enjoyed writing songs and poems for her own amusement, a hobby that continued even after the family moved to Lowell following her father's death. Larcom's mother ran a boardinghouse for migrant millworkers, and after just a few years in Lowell's schools, Lucy joined her older sisters as one of the thousands of so-called mill girls. At age eleven, she worked as a doffer, exchanging empty bobbins for new ones on the massive, room-sized weaving looms. In her autobiography, *A New England Girlhood*, she writes:

> *The novelty of it made it seem easy, and it really was not hard, just to change the bobbins on the spinning frames every three quarters of an hour or so, with half a dozen other littler girls who were doing the same thing.*

However, her sense of the new job being a fun form of make-believe disappeared when she graduated from grammar school but was obliged to remain in the mills instead of continuing to high school.

While Lowell's mill owners certainly profited from exploiting these young women's acceptance of longer hours and lower wages than their adult counterparts, it was also essential that the mills help protect their employees' reputations and their own by enforcing strict moral standards. Unlike the Larcom sisters, most mill girls were in Lowell on their own, having come to the city as an alternative to farm work. They lived in company-owned boardinghouses, where strict curfews and church attendance were mandatory. There were also ample opportunities for education—after all, despite their unique position as wage-earning bank account holders, these girls would need to grow up to become respectable wives and mothers.

With financial support from the mill, Larcom and some of her fellow mill girls started the *Lowell Offering* in 1840, a newspaper publishing stories, poems and letters written by the girls. The mill heavily promoted the magazine as an example of the ways in which

Lucy Larcom, circa 1880.

millwork, far from being rough and degrading, could actually be enlightening and edifying for these young women. Larcom, at age fourteen, received national and international attention as the editor and most frequent contributor to this unique *Offering*. Among her literary admirers was the poet John Greenleaf Whittier, whom she met when he edited the *Middlesex Standard*; the two maintained a friendship for the rest of their lives.

Larcom left the mills in 1846 to travel with a married sister to Illinois, where she taught school for a few years and continued her own education. By the time she returned to Massachusetts in 1852, life at the mills had changed. The workforce was no longer fueled by Yankee farm girls, but by recent Irish immigrants. The mills were less invested in protecting and educating these girls, let alone ensuring that they would become upstanding moral adults, and the world of the mill girl truly did become more troubling and exploitative than ever. Larcom did not return to the mills; instead, she spent the next ten years teaching. After retiring, and for the next thirty years of her life, she devoted herself to writing, as well as editing, the children's magazine *Our Young Folks* with Mary Abigail Dodge.

PLACES TO SEE

Larcom Park, parallel to the canal that runs along Dutton Street, Lowell
This park, popular with students on break from nearby Lowell High School, runs along the canal that helped power Lowell's textile mills. Today, many of Lowell's arts and ethnic festivals take place in and around this small green space in the midst of Lowell's urban downtown.

American Textile History Museum, 491 Dutton Street, Lowell
In addition to exhibitions of historic and contemporary fabric and fiber arts, the museum also tells the history of Lowell's mills and the men, women and children who worked there. Its collections contain a wealth of information about textile art, factory architecture, textile production, technological invention, labor history, industrial organization and the everyday life of mill towns.

JACK KEROUAC (1922–1969)

*The "Beat Generation" was born disillusioned; it takes for granted the
imminence of war, the barrenness of politics and the hostility of the
rest of society. It is not even impressed by (although it never pretends to
scorn) material well being (as distinguished from materialism). It does
not know what refuge it is seeking, but it is seeking.*
—*Gilbert Millstein, reviewing* On the Road *in the* New York
Times, *September 5, 1957*

Lowell's prosperity had already begun to wane by the time Jean-
Louis Kerouac was born in 1922. Raised in a working-class French
Canadian family, the boy who would become the greatest of the Beat
Generation writers originally planned to put himself through college
on a football scholarship and enter the insurance business. He did
manage the first half of that plan, playing well enough on his high
school team to earn a scholarship to Columbia University in New
York City. Injury and arguments with the coach left him sidelined
and disillusioned, and it wasn't long before he dropped out.

It was during this time that he met the writers with whom he
would be affiliated for the rest of his life, and for posterity, as "the
Beats." Although he never spent a significant amount of time living
in Lowell again, the city and his French Canadian roots remained
a strong presence in his mind and his work. In his story "October
in the Railroad Earth," in the 1953 volume *Lonesome Traveler*, he
describes San Francisco railroad yards:

> *And everything is pouring in—the switching moves of boxcars in
> that little alley, which is so much like the alleys of Lowell, and
> I hear far off in the sense of coming night that engine calling
> our mountains.*

In his first published novel, *Town and City* (1950), Lowell
is renamed Galloway, and Kerouac rechristens himself with

the pseudonym Dulouz. Fourteen more books, including the posthumously published *Atop an Underwood* (1999), would make up what scholars call "the Dulouz legend," and five of these deal with his early life in Lowell. Arranged chronologically by the time in Kerouac's life that they cover, although not necessarily by the date written or published, these are *Visions of Gerard* (1963), *Doctor Sax* (1959), *The Town and the City* (1950), *Maggie Cassidy* (1959) and *The Vanity of Dulouz* (1968).

PLACES TO SEE

Edson Cemetery, Lowell
Near the city's edge, and therefore a good place to start this brief tour of landmarks in the Beat poet's life, is Edson Cemetery, where the poet is buried next to his wife. Heading south on 3A/Gorham Street, enter the cemetery by turning right at the gatekeeper's house, shortly before the street splits at the Citgo station. Turn left and proceed to the cemetery road marked Seventh Street. Kerouac's grave is near the corner of Seventh and Lincoln Streets, at the center of section ninety-four. The grass around his grave has been worn away by visitors, many of whom leave candles, pens, packs of cigarettes and scraps of their own poetry in remembrance of the Beat Generation's most recognizable voice.

Jack Kerouac Park, Lowell
Downtown, Lowell celebrates this famous son with a number of landmarks, most notably Jack Kerouac Park on Bridge Street near where it intersects with French Street. With the former Kitson textile mill in the background, this small willow tree–ringed park features large granite obelisks engraved with passages from Kerouac's work. Artist Ben Woitena designed the site with input from Kerouac's wife Stella, and the park was dedicated on June 25, 1988. Excerpts from his most well-known and widely read work, *On the Road*, stand side by side with passages that pay homage to the hometown that was always prominent in Kerouac's writing.

Jack Kerouac Park, Lowell.

Kerouac's Birthplace, 9 Lupine Road, Lowell

The house where Kerouac was born in 1922 is marked with a plaque from the city's historical commission. Located at the edge of the working-class Centralville neighborhood, the brown house with yellow trim is much like any of the nearby two-family homes—and it still is a private two-family home—but neighbors don't mind the occasional Beat buffs who drive by to get a glimpse of where one of their favorite authors came into the world.

66 West Street, Lowell

One of nine residences that the family had in Lowell, they moved here after the death of Jack's older brother Gerard from complications of rheumatic fever. They lived here for three years, which was about as long as Kerouac ever lived in one place over his entire life. Especially in the novel *Doctor Sax*, Kerouac recalls frequent visitors and parties at the upstairs apartment.

Self-Guided Tour

For those interested in a much more in-depth tour of Kerouac sites in Lowell—both from the author's life and his work—the Jack Kerouac's Lowell project offers three different walking tour pamphlets, created by Brian Foye and Mark Hemenway. Visit ecommunity.uml.edu/jklowell/index.html or the National Historical Park Visitor Center in the Market Mills, Lowell, to print out or pick up a copy.

A North Shore & Merrimack Valley Bookstore Sampler

This list is by no means comprehensive—it includes just a few of my favorite bookstores in and around the North Shore. If you're interested in keeping up on nearby literary events and the newest titles by local authors, the staff at independent bookstores can be some of your best resources.

Gloucester

Ten Pound Island Books, 77 Langsford Street
Local author Gregory Gibson has run this small antiquarian and used bookstore in the Lanesville section of Gloucester since 1976. It specializes in old and rare nautical books, but you'll find books on all kinds of maritime and local subjects, as well as extremely knowledgeable staff.

The Bookstore of Gloucester, 61 Main Street
The selection here includes currently popular titles in both fiction and nonfiction, with a bent toward nautical titles and left-leaning

activism. Their magazine section is one of the most well-stocked north of Boston, with a large selection of small-run and urban culture titles.

ESSEX

White Elephant Antiques Shop, 101 John Wise Avenue
On Route 133, also known as John Wise Avenue, and housed in a big red barn, the White Elephant Antiques Shop offers the kind of organized chaos that antique hunters love, with furniture, art and bins of vintage jewelry. Bookstalls outside bring a taste of Paris's legendary Left Bank booksellers' market to New England and serve as a picturesque place to hunt for that perfect rainy day vacation read. The shop is right next to the former site of John Wise's home—you'll notice a marker in front of the hedges that surround the current private home.

Book stalls line the wall outdoors at the White Elephant Antiques shop in Essex.

MARBLEHEAD

Spirit of '76, 107 Pleasant Street
This independent bookstore has been a staple in Marblehead since 1965. The selection includes currently popular fiction and nonfiction alongside nautical and maritime history and a large kids' room. Spirit of '76 is known for its customer service, and even the local college students working summer jobs there are avid readers and quick with suggestions. The store is also the headquarters for more than three dozen local book groups, whose current selections are on display—great for discovering an overlooked title and getting a glimpse into what the community is reading.

NEWBURYPORT

Jabberwocky, at the Tannery 50 Water Street
For more than thirty years, the Jabberwocky bookstore has catered to passionate readers on the North Shore. With a large selection of works by local authors and events most Friday evenings, it is a place for both browsing and socializing.

BEVERLY

The Book Shop, 40 West Street, Beverly Farms
Browsing the various rooms in this airy home turned bookshop is like wandering through a friend's vast library. Book recommendations

from the staff and fellow patrons are left throughout the store on sticky notes, and cozy wicker furniture in the front room provides a sunny spot to sit and page through your discoveries. Immediately to the left after entering is a small but carefully selected section of works by local authors—including a full shelf of work by John Updike—and the staff at the Book Shop are happy to recommend and order anything you're looking for.

WENHAM

Banbury Cross Children's Bookshop, 162 R Main Street
With book talks for children and parents alike, storytelling, language classes for kids and a staff of children's literature experts, Banbury Cross is perfect for bibliophile parents who want to pass that passion along to their kids. The booksellers can help suggest titles for reluctant readers, books that complement school projects, series that feature whatever a child's current obsession is and perennial favorites that parents remember from their own childhood.

SALEM

Cornerstone Books, 45 Lafayette Street
Cornerstone carries a wide selection of books, both serious and silly, and is a great place to start your exploration of witch hysteria and its repercussions or to pick up a souvenir to continue your exploration. The "Witch City" section of the store's website at www.cornerstonebooks-salem.com is frequently updated with new titles about the city, its history, fictional magic and contemporary Wiccan culture. Cornerstone also hosts frequent author events and

book signings and is home base for Grub Street North, the North Shore chapter of the Boston-based writers' workshop. Its monthly roundtable is designed to give writers an inside glimpse into the world of publishing.

Peabody Essex Museum, East India Square (161 Essex Street)
The bookstore section of the Peabody Essex Museum's shop is a small but well-selected browser's delight. It's one of the best spaces in town to peruse gorgeous art books that relate to the museum's international collection, as well as North Shore history.

Derby Square Books, 215 Essex Street
Derby Square Books is not for the claustrophobic or control freak, but for those who enjoy the serendipity of discovering new titles among towering piles of books, this shop is a blast. That's not to say that there's no order in the chaos—if you know just what book you're looking for, the owner is great at locating exact titles and helping you dig them out from the bottom of a stack.

ANDOVER

Andover Bookstore, 89R Main Street, Andover
The Andover Bookstore boasts of being the second oldest in America. It began in 1809, when Mark Newman resigned as principal of Phillips Academy to become the academy's bookseller. Through a few changes of ownership and location, the store continued to be the primary source of books for the Phillips Academy community and housed the Andover Press until 1960. Today, the store is in a renovated barn with a book-filled balcony and comfortable chairs near a working fireplace. Not surprisingly, it is a perfect place to visit on a gray New England day. The store hosts author events most Thursday evenings.

Notes

Preface

1. Thompson, *Essays and Reviews*, 569.
2. Ipswich to Ipswich: History through Art, http://
   www.ipswichtoipswich.com/historicalconnections/
   colonistsfromipswichuk.html.

Gloucester

3. Tolan, "Gloucester's Legacy of Loss."
4. Swigart, *Olson's Gloucester*, 5.
5. Ellemen, *Virginia Lee Burton*, 23.
6. Mirakove, Nguyen interview.
7. Stormont, "Vincent Ferrini."
8. Joe Garland, e-mail to the author, October 22, 2008.

Ipswich

9. Tyler, *History of American Literature*, 231.

10. Edney and Cimburek, "Telling the Traumatic Truth."
11. "View from the Catacombs," *Time*, April 26, 1968. Accessed online at http://www.time.com/time/magazine/article/0,9171,838313-1,00.html.
12. Frost, "Updike, John."
13. De Bellis, *John Updike Encyclopedia*, 470; Cheshire, *What Makes Rabbit Run?*

ESSEX

14. Fleisher, "Antiquing Destination."
15. Long, *American Ideal*.

NAHANT

16. Longfellow, *Life of Henry Wadsworth Longfellow*, 317.
17. Ibid., 355.
18. "The Burnt Longfellow Cottage."

AMESBURY

19. Letter to F.H. Underwood, in Perry, *Park-street Papers*, 274.
20. Robinson, "Inside the Whittier Home."

SALISBURY

21. Essex Natural Heritage Commission, Reconnaissance Report.

NEWBURYPORT

22. Bell, *Marquand*.
23. Heffner, *A Documentary History*, 129.

24. Richard, "Harriet Spofford."
25. Martin, *Cambridge Companion*, 186.
26. Ibid.
27. Yardley, "Second Reading," C01.
28. Bell, *Marquand*.
29. Spaulding, "Martini-Age Victorian."
30. Stuart Deane, "A Park."
31. Robert Birnbaum, interview with Andre Dubus III, 2000, http://www.identitytheory.com/people/birnbaum3.html.
32. Ibid.

PEABODY

33. Tise, *American Counterrevolution*, 186.
34. Bolton, *Elizabeth Whitman Mystery*, 29.

DANVERS

35. Kennedy, *John Greenleaf Whittier*, 153–54.

BEVERLY

36. Garland, *North Shore*, 20.
37. Addison, *Lucy Larcom*, 188.
38. Harold Laski, Review of *The Happy Profession* by Ellery Sedgwick, *New England Quarterly* 20, no. 1 (March 1947), 114–17.
39. Davison, "The First Three Poems."

SALEM

40. Barry, *Lace Reader*.
41. Larcom, *A New England Girlhood*, 94.
42. Parrington, *Colonial Mind*.

43. Bentley et al., *Diary of William Bentley*, vol. 1, 140.
44. James, *Hawthorne*, 52.
45. Tolles et al., *Architecture in Salem*, 196.
46. "Prospectus of Mathews Normal Training School," 141.
47. Alcott, *Journals of Bronson Alcott*, 107–08.
48. Hileman, "Jones Very."
49. Gura, *American Transcendentalism*, 288.

Andover

50. Warner, "Story of Uncles Tom's Cabin," 311–21.
51. Biggs, *Women's Words*, 113.
52. "Elizabeth Stuart Phelps."

Haverhill

53. "Can All Come Green Again?"
54. Behlen, "Winfield Townley Scott."
55. Sullivan, "Now 60 Year Old."
56. Ibid.

Lawrence

57. Greater Lawrence Family Health Center brochure.

BIBLIOGRAPHY

Addison, Daniel Dulany, ed. *Lucy Larcom: Life, Letters, and Diary*. Boston: Houghton, Mifflin and Co., 1894.

Alcott, Amos Bronson, and Odell Shepard, eds. *The Journals of Bronson Alcott*. Boston: Little, Brown, 1938.

Barry, Brunonia. *The Lace Reader* promotional website. Harper Collins, 2008. http://www.lacereader.com/main.php.

Behlen, Charles William. "Winfield Townley Scott." *The Literary Encyclopedia*, September 9, 2006. http://www.litencyc.com/php/speople.php?rec=true&UID=3985.

Bell, Millicent. *Marquand: An American Life*. Boston: Little, Brown, 1979.

Bentley, William, with Joseph Gilbert Waters, Marguerite Dalrymple and Alice G. Waters. *The Diary of William Bentley, D.D.* Salem, MA: The Essex Institute, 1905.

Biggs, Mary, comp. *Women's Words: The Columbia Book of Quotations by Women*. New York: Columbia University Press, 1996.

Bolton, Charles Knowles. *The Elizabeth Whitman Mystery at the Old Bell Tavern in Danvers*. Peabody, MA: Peabody Historical Society, 1912.

Boston Transcript. "The Burnt Longfellow Cottage." May 31, 1896.

Cheshire, David, director. *What Makes Rabbit Run?* Videocassette. Boulder, CO: Centre Productions, 1985.

Davison, Peter. "The First Three Poems and One That Got Away." *Atlantic Monthly*, January 31, 2006. Available online at http://www.theatlantic.com/doc/199604u/frost-intro.

Deane, Stuart. "A park where past and future also play." *Boston Globe*, September 14, 2008.

De Bellis, Jack. *The John Updike Encyclopedia*. Westport, CT: Greenwood Publishing Group, 2000.

Edney, Matthew H., and Susan Cimburek. "Telling the Traumatic Truth: William Hubbard's Narrative of King Philip's War and His 'Map of New-England.'" *William and Mary Quarterly* 61, no. 2 (2004).

"Elizabeth Stuart Phelps." *Old and Sold Antiques Digest*. http://www.oldandsold.com/articles27n/women-authors-1.shtml.

Ellemen, Barbara. *Virginia Lee Burton*. Boston: Houghton, Mifflin and Co., Children's Books, 2002.

Essex Natural Heritage Commission, Massachusetts Heritage Landscape Inventory Program. Salisbury Reconnaissance Report, May 2005. Available online at www.essexheritage.org/heritagelandscapes/salisbury.pdf.

Fleisher, Noah. "Antiquing Destination: Essex, Massachusetts," *New England Antiques Journal* (November 2006). Available online at http://www.antiquesjournal.com/pages04/Monthly_pages/nov06/tour.html.

Frost, Adam. "Updike, John." *Literature Online* biography. http://gateway.proquest.com.ezp-prod1.hul.harvard.edu/openurl?ctx_ver=Z39.88-2003&xri:pqil:res_ver=0.2&res_id=xri:lion-us&rft_id=xri:lion:rec:ref:3213.

Garland, Joseph E. *The Gloucester Guide*. Rockport, MA: Protean Press, 1990.

———. *The North Shore*. Beverly, MA: Commonwealth Editions, 1998.

Greater Lawrence Family Health Center brochure, 2006. http://www.cdc.gov/reach/pdf/MA_Greater_Lawrence.pdf.

Gura, Philip F. *American Transcendentalism: A History*. New York: Hill and Wang, 2007.

Heffner, Richard D., ed. *A Documentary History of the United States*. New York: Signet Classic, 2002.

Hileman, Bryan. "Jones Very." *American Transcendentalism Web*. Virginia Commonwealth University. http://www.vcu.edu/ engweb/transcendentalism/authors/very.

James, Henry. *Hawthorne*. New York: Harper and Brothers, 1901.

Kennedy, William Sloane. *John Greenleaf Whittier*. Chicago: The Werner Company, 1895.

Larcom, Lucy. *A New England Girlhood: Outlined from Memory*. Boston: Houghton, Mifflin and Co., 1889.

Long, Hamilton Abert. *The American Ideal of 1776: The Twelve Basic American Principles*. N.p.: Your Heritage Books, 1976. Available online at http://www.lexrex.com/enlightened/AmericanIdeal.

Longfellow, Samuel, ed. *Life of Henry Wadsworth Longfellow: With Extracts from His Journals and Correspondence*. Boston: Ticknor and Company, 1886.

Martin, Wendy. *The Cambridge Companion to Emily Dickinson*. Cambridge, MA: Cambridge University Press, 2002.

Mirakove, Carol. Interview with Hoa Nguyen. *Readme*, no. 2 (winter 2000). http://home.jps.net/~nada/nguyen.htm.

Parrington, Vernon. *The Colonial Mind 1620–1800*. New York: Harcourt, 1955. Accessed online at http://xroads.virginia.edu/ ~Hyper/Parrington/vol1/bk01_02_ch01.html.

Perry, Bliss. *Park-street Papers*. New York: Houghton, Mifflin & Co., 1908.

"Prospectus of Mathews Normal Training School, Portland, Oregon." In Eisenmann, Linda. *Historical Dictionary of Women's Education*. Westport, CT: Greenwood Publishing Group, 1998.

Richard, Thelma Shinn. "Harriet Spofford." In *The Heath Anthology of American Literature*. 5th edition. Edited by Paul Lauter. Available online at http://college.cengage.com/english/ lauter/heath/4e/students/author_pages/late_nineteenth/ spofford_ha.html.

Robinson, Denis J. "Inside the Whittier Home." *SeacoastNH.com*, 2000. http://www.seacoastnh.com/dct/whittier1.html.

Spaulding, Martha. "Martini-Age Victorian." *Atlantic* (May 2004).

Stormont, Craig. "Vincent Ferrini: The Initiations." *Big Bridge*, no. 9 (2003). http://www.bigbridge.org/issue9/ferrini2.htm.

Sullivan, Mark. "Now 60 Year Old, Archie Has Roots Reaching to Haverhill." *Boston Globe*, December 30, 2001, Northwest Weekly section, 6.

Swigart, Lynn. *Olson's Gloucester*. Baton Rouge: Louisiana State University Press, 1980.

Thompson, Garry Richard, ed. *Essays and Reviews by Edgar Allan Poe*. New York: Library of America, 1984.

Time. "Can All Come Green Again?" August 21, 1964. Available online at http://www.time.com/time/magazine/article/0,9171,876071,00.html?promoid=googlep.

Tise, Larry E. *The American Counterrevolution: A Retreat from Liberty, 1783–1800*. Mechanicsburg, PA: Stackpole Books, 1998.

Tolan, Sandy. "Gloucester's Legacy of Loss." *Living on Earth*, WBUR, February 5, 1999. Transcript available at http://www.loe.org/shows/shows.htm?programID=99-P13-00006.

Tolles, Bryant Franklin Jr., Bryant F. Tolles, Carolyn K. Tolles and Paul F. Norton. *Architecture in Salem: An Illustrated Guide*. Lebanon, NH: University Press of New England, 2004.

Tyler, Moses Coit. *A History of American Literature During the Colonial Time*. Vol. 1. New York: G.P. Putnam's Sons, 1897.

Warner, Charles Dudley. "The Story of Uncles Tom's Cabin." *Atlantic Monthly* 78 (1896).

Yardley, Jonathan. "Second Reading: John Marquand, Zinging WASPs With a Smooth Sting." *Washington Post*, February 20, 2003, C01.

INDEX

Visit us at
www.historypress.net